Engagement **Matters**
Personalised learning for Grades 3 to 6

Kathy Walker
and
Shona Bass

Published in 2025 by Amba Press, Melbourne, Australia
www.ambapress.com.au

First published in 2011 by ACER Press, an imprint of
Australian Council for Educational Research Ltd

© 2025 Kathy Walker and Shona Bass

Photographs with thanks to Penbank School, Manchester Primary School, St Clements of Rome Primary School, Gibbs St Primary School and ACER India.

This book is copyright. All rights reserved. Except under the conditions described in the Copyright Act 1968 of Australia and subsequent amendments, and any exceptions permitted under the current statutory licence scheme administered by Copyright Agency Limited (www.copyright.com.au), no part of this publication may be reproduced, stored in a retrieval system, transmitted, broadcast or communicated in any form or by any means, optical, digital, electronic, mechanical, photocopying, recording or otherwise, without the written permission of the publisher.

Copying of the blackline master pages
The purchasing educational institution and its staff are permitted to make copies of the pages marked as blackline master pages, beyond their rights under the Act, provided that:
1. the number of copies does not exceed the number reasonably required by the educational institution to satisfy its teaching purposes;
2. copies are made only by reprographic means (photocopying), not by electronic/digital means, and not stored or transmitted;
3. copies are not sold or lent; and
4. every copy made clearly shows the footnote ('Copyright © Kathy Walker and Shona Bass 2011').

For those pages not marked as blackline master pages the normal copying limits in the Act, as described above, apply.

Edited by Elisa Webb
Cover design by JAC Design

ISBN: 9781923569065 (pbk)
ISBN: 9781923569072 (ebk)

A catalogue record for this book is available from the National Library of Australia.

Contents

Preface iv

Chapter 1 Teaching and learning in the 21st century: Engagement, motivation and sustained learning 1

Introduction 2
Key components required for teaching and learning in the 21st century 3
Moving into the next stage of schooling: A developmental perspective 5
Defining the differences between curriculum, pedagogy, philosophy and values 8
Summary 11

Chapter 2 The Walker Learning Approach Grades 3–6 13

Introduction 14
Key principles 14
Key components 15
How a day and week looks and operates 26
Summary 29

Chapter 3 Recommendations for schools introducing the Walker Learning Approach 31

Introduction 32
Successful implementation of a teaching and learning philosophy 32
Summary 39

Chapter 4 Education research projects 41

Introduction 42
ERPs at a glance 43
Unpacking ERPs 43
Understanding the ERP process 45
Schedule of ERP events 48
The expo 51
Summary 53

Chapter 5 Planning and documentation 55

Introduction 56
WLA planning tools 56
Summary 63

Chapter 6 Assessment and reporting 65

Introduction 66
Meaningful assessment and reporting 67
WLA assessment 68
WLA reporting 70
Other issues related to assessment and reporting 72
Summary 74

Chapter 7 Case studies 75

Introduction 76
Developing the ERP proposal 76
Summary 81

Chapter 8 Troubleshooting and frequently asked questions 83

Appendices 89
    Term Subject Focus and Key Learning Intentions 90
    Statement of Intent 91
    Focus Student Roster 92
    Clinic Group Timetable 93
    Clinic Group Sign-up Sheets 94
    Individual Record (Teacher's Notes) 96
    Individual Record (Student/Parent Contributions) 97
    ERP Student Proposal 98
    ERP Contract 99
    ERP Assessment Guide 100
    Learning Intentions (Student Version) 101

These appendices are also provided as downloadable interactive files.

References 102
Index 104

Preface

The Walker Learning Approach (WLA) is being implemented across the first three years of over 1000 schools throughout Australia; from Arnhem Land to Tasmania and everywhere in between. The success of this pedagogy is underpinned by the authentic engagement of children combined with child-centred learning. This philosophical approach to teaching and learning provides an exciting, interesting and engaging learning environment for all children regardless of their socioeconomic, cultural, geographical or family background. The teacher authentically 'teaches to the child' whoever they are, wherever they are and whatever their background.

The success of the WLA in the junior years has provided the platform for Kathy Walker and Shona Bass to work with schools and teachers to develop a pedagogy based on this philosophy that is developmentally appropriate for the upper years of primary school (Grades 3–6). This provides a more seamless and consistent set of practices for teaching and learning as children move from Grade 2 into their middle and upper primary years. It is an exciting stage in education to witness schools and teachers embracing an even broader range of teaching and learning strategies that truly engage, motivate and excite children.

Engagement Matters is designed to provide information and strategies for school communities that are interested in implementing the WLA in the middle and upper primary years. The book is a continuation of the key principles and pedagogical philosophies documented in *Play Matters* (WLA over the first three years of school). *Engagement Matters* covers different key strategies that match the developmental and learning needs and strengths of children as they move into these next years of their education.

The book is divided into chapters and sections which cover specific issues, recommendations and strategies to support not only teachers but also leaders, parents, children and schools as they move to implement the WLA.

Chapter 1: Teaching and learning in the 21st century

This chapter highlights the range of skills—such as problem solving, initiative, independence and interdependence—that are required to lead a fulfilling and productive life in an increasingly complex world. It also highlights the major issues related to teaching and learning across the middle primary years and associated implications for schools in developing a clear philosophy and matching pedagogy that will enable effective implementation of the WLA.

It includes the following discussions:

- key components required for teaching and learning in the 21st century

- key questions facing middle and upper primary educators

- moving into the next stage of schooling

- developmentally appropriate practice

- clarifying the differences between curriculum, pedagogy, philosophy and values

- the importance of a whole-school philosophy.

Chapter 2: The Walker Learning Approach Grades 3–6

This chapter provides a complete outline and description of what the key features of the WLA are across Grades 3–6, and how it works in a classroom and within a teaching team. It provides specific details on each main component of the approach and how it links to all areas of teaching and learning, including room set-up, the communication board, clinic groups and class meetings.

Chapter 3: Recommendations for schools introducing the Walker Learning Approach

This chapter provides recommendations and strategies for the actual understandings and processes required by a school community or team as they deal with issues of change when implementing the WLA. It also offers practical recommendations for the steps and strategies needed in order to go on to implement the WLA successfully and to ensure a sustained and effective teaching and learning model.

Chapter 4: Education research projects

This chapter provides a detailed unpacking of education research projects, including detailed descriptions of each element of the ERP, how to introduce them to the students and how to develop proposals, contracts and other aspects of the ERP.

Chapter 5: Planning and documentation

This chapter provides explanations and examples of the intentional, rigorous and detailed planning that underpins the success of the WLA. It unpacks examples of the range of ways that planning, documenting learning and observations can be used as part of the teaching and learning process.

Chapter 6: Assessment and reporting

This chapter reviews what meaningful assessment and reporting really is and how it can be achieved and disseminated to students, parents and the school. It provides ideas for enhancing more holistic reporting strategies that reflect deeper achievements of students than just literacy and numeracy results.

Chapter 7: Case studies

This chapter provides some real life examples of the development of ERP proposals and how teachers and students can work together during ERP times.

Chapter 8: Troubleshooting and frequently asked questions

This chapter includes questions, challenges and issues that arise from time to time in some teams or communities and provides some suggestions and strategies to overcome them.

Appendices

This section includes templates and pro formas for schools to photocopy and use as part of the WLA. Interactive electronic versions are also supplied on the CD attached to the back of the book.

Chapter 1

Teaching and learning in the 21st century: Engagement, motivation and sustained learning

'The object of education is to prepare the young to educate themselves throughout their lives.'

Robert Maynard Hutchins

Introduction

We believe and have witnessed through the Walker Learning Approach (WLA) that when students are provided with specific opportunities that empower them and provide them with opportunities to make some of their own decisions, they step up and engage in highly meaningful and sustained ways.

Children have traditionally reflected increased dissatisfaction with and disengagement from their learning in the middle and upper years of primary (DEET 2002). We want to set children up in the middle primary years to succeed, thrive and flourish rather than just cope, struggle or fail. As they transition into the upper primary years, we want children to engage with a seamless set of strategies that build upon their first three years of school; that will provide continuity, consistency and opportunities for individual interests.

The WLA is based on the concept of developmentally appropriate practices. Programs based on this theory have taken a variety of shapes and forms over the past five decades and primarily have an emphasis on acknowledging that both developmental and environmental influences impact on each individual's ability and timing of learning. The WLA has been designed to reflect the range of cultural, demographic, economic and social factors that are part of education systems across the Western world. The program seeks to ensure that classrooms are filled with highly motivated children who are learning how to learn with a mix of active investigation and formalised instruction alongside opportunities for greater levels of decision-making, choice, active participation and a wide range of mediums in which to explore, learn and acquire skills.

As children move through the early childhood years (0–8 years), the transition from preschool into primary school requires teachers to ensure that many of the teaching and learning strategies children experienced as preschoolers are maintained and built upon. These eight years of maturation, growth and brain development require the young learner to not only have instruction in literacy and numeracy but also lots of concrete, hands-on, real materials and resources to interact and construct with. Alongside the recognition that children are more highly motivated to learn and sustain their own learning if they are engaged through opportunities to make authentic choices, ensuring a seamless transition between preschool and the first years of school was one of the original aims of the WLA.

The transition between Grades 2 and 3 is a significant pathway into another part of child development. Children move out of the unique characteristics that define the early childhood years and into a slightly higher level of thinking, processing and understanding. The WLA seeks to ensure that children moving from their early childhood classrooms into the higher grades are provided with a seamless and consistent set of practices and strategies that maximise engagement and motivation. We want children in these years to have a sense of empowerment and ownership of their own learning, to view the learning process as meaningful to their lives now and for the future. We want them to have a range of choices within the limits set by the teacher and to learn to identity some of their own learning needs as well as to continue to build upon their self-esteem and identity.

The importance of consistent teaching and learning practices across a school community is only now becoming more apparent, accepted and acknowledged in mainstream schools. It is important for children and their families to be clear about the teaching and learning strategies and philosophies that are used across the school and that these strategies and philosophies are consistent, shared and constantly reflected upon. The old days of teachers being locked away in their individual classrooms should be well and truly over! The old comment, 'I just like to teach my own way, and it doesn't matter how the teacher next door teaches', is inappropriate. There is so much important research that highlights the need for clarity of philosophy and consistent practices right across a school (Livingston, McClain & DeSpain 1995; Weinstock, Starr & Fazzaro 1974).

We often make the comment that, 'It is not the child who must constantly adapt and change to different teaching methodologies, it is the teachers and the school community as a whole that are required to ensure consistency of philosophy and pedagogy'.

Some teachers and even some leaders of schools are sometimes confused by this. They feel that each teacher has a right to do their own thing in their own way. They fail to understand or accept that as educators we must provide a consistent set of strategies, and that we now have access to a range of significant and highly valid research which can guide and support schools in developing their teaching and learning approaches (Summers 1994). Obviously each teacher maintains their own unique personality, and translates some of the practices and philosophy into their own manner. However, it is imperative that school communities provide consistent teaching and learning across the school which reflects and directly and consistently translates the school's educational philosophy.

The WLA provides a platform of evidence, research and practical strategies to schools which seek high levels of student engagement and motivation; and for students to be independent learners who are acquiring skills, not just 'content'.

The content of curriculum (literacy, numeracy, science, health, history, etc.) will always be found in curriculum framework documents, which change regularly. The WLA works in all states and territories and easily incorporates the wide range of content in each framework document, and the planning ensures that all requirements are met. The emphasis of the WLA, however, is not on the 'what' (curriculum) but most importantly the 'how' (pedagogy).

In this chapter we take the time to discuss the real and authentic elements of educating children in the 21st century, and developmentally appropriate practice for Grades 3–6 is explained more fully. Aspects of education that are needed to set children up to be successful learners, to know how to learn, to love learning, to be resilient, to problem-solve, to think laterally and to view life as an opportunity to learn no matter how old they may be are addressed. The often misunderstood terminology related to curriculum, pedagogy, values and philosophies is clarified. The chapter concludes with the contextual importance of leadership within the school and how that may influence the learning journey of the school community.

Key components required for teaching and learning in the 21st century

Children need to be provided with a solid foundation of skill acquisition and to develop a range of thinking and research abilities in order to learn how to learn. It is our responsibility as educators to ensure that children are provided with these learning opportunities. We cannot possibly teach the content or knowledge of all there currently is to know in the world, or predict what information will be necessary in the future. We can, however, provide learning environments that offer lots of practice in how to make decisions, initiate ideas, persist, find out, try again, take risks, explore and research in a range of ways that relate to children's own unique interests and endeavours; and to balance this with the areas of content and information that we as educators wish to introduce and provide.

Teaching and learning in the 21st century requires acknowledgement that successful education needs to provide a set of fundamental foundation skills that are transferable *and* adaptable *for whatever the future holds.*

The results of research indicate that there are a number of key components required for successful learning to occur and to be sustained and transferable into the future (Time, Learning and Afterschool Task Force 2007). These include:

- intrinsic motivation

- relationship building and trust between students and staff

- empowerment and ownership of the learning

- engagement through authentic and relevant interests of children

- acquiring the skills of effective research, problem-solving, risk taking and resilience

- an emphasis on skills rather than knowledge or content

- learning how to learn
- a positive and realistic sense of self
- resilience
- working independently and interdependently.

The results of research also identify a number of factors conducive to student engagement (Bandura 1997):

- Students are more likely to engage and find learning meaningful if they have some ownership of their learning and the learning environment.
- Students require some opportunities for their learning to be personalised, thus ensuring that the particular strengths, needs and interests of each student are best met.
- Students require opportunities to contribute to their learning, to make ideas and to offer suggestions that are factored in legitimately as part of the teaching and learning.

Most educators would agree with the points above, but there is vast diversity in the interpretation and application of these aspects of learning. For example, authentic and relevant interests require educators to personalise as many aspects of learning, projects and expectations as possible. Setting out a scope and sequence chart with predetermined topics years ahead of meeting the class of children (or before they even begin school) does not provide a personalised opportunity for students to become engaged in learning through their own authentic interests; it presumes that all students must somehow adapt their interests to fit the current topic. We explain throughout *Engagement Matters* that in the WLA, topics and predetermined units of inquiry are not necessary. The WLA's starting point is the authentic interests of the child alongside learning intentions from curriculum frameworks. By moving away from the starting point of a topic or unit of inquiry, the WLA immediately opens up a greater range of opportunities for students to have their own interests embedded within the areas of information and skills that schools are required to meet.

The WLA not only ensures that curriculum obligations for content and skills are maintained and enhanced but that this is achieved by teaching strategies that truly and effectively engage, empower and provide greater ownership and choice for students. It is after all, the students' learning that is most important, not educators' predetermined interests or topics.

The methodology of engagement, motivation, teaching and learning is the foundation the WLA is built upon. Through our work over the past 15 years we have collected data to ensure that not only are students motivated by and engaged with a range of authentic learning experiences but that literacy, numeracy, reading and writing are enhanced and sustained through this approach.

The WLA is an evidence-based pedagogy. Our own studies across years P–2, as well as data collected by schools for state and federal purposes indicate that children's oral language, attendance, punctuality, general eagerness and engagement with school and learning have all increased significantly under the WLA (Walker 2009). We have noted that while both boys and girls have higher levels of engagement in the WLA, it is particularly pleasing to see that young boys—who often display behavioural challenges—are strongly engaged and less prone to behavioural problems.

The philosophy and implementation of the WLA consistently demonstrate that engaging children is the first fundamental 'must' for successful teaching and learning. Underpinning this fundamental must is the understanding that compliance does not equate to engagement—engagement represents children being truly and authentically interested and excited in what they are doing and that it is real, relevant and meaningful to them as unique individuals.

The WLA seeks to ensure that engagement, motivation, consistency of practice and a shared philosophy across a school all work in the interests of students to maximise each individual child's opportunity to find the learning environment truly relevant, meaningful, exciting and successful.

Key questions facing middle and upper primary educators

There are a number of additional and different challenges that face educators in how to engage, sustain motivation and personalise learning for children as they make the transition from their early childhood grades into the middle and upper primary years. Some of the key questions we ask include how do we:

- engage students in meaningful rather than tokenistic ways?

- help students develop responsible decision-making skills and independence as well as interdependence in their learning?

- motivate students to self motivate and take some responsibility for their own learning and behaviour?

- cover the content and issues expected from governments in ways that are relevant, meaningful and useful to students?

- avoid disenfranchising and disengaging students?

- build and sustain positive and trusting relationships between students and teachers/schools?

- provide a set of consistent strategies between the early, middle and upper years of primary school to ensure a seamless transition from one grade to the next?

- provide opportunities for children to have a real voice and contribute towards their own learning?

- provide opportunities for students to develop self reflection, evaluation and self assessment?

- provide meaningful and authentic assessment and reporting strategies that are far deeper than standardised tests?

- construct the learning environment; what does it need to look and feel like to engage and promote a sense of ownership? How can it reflect the changes in development, maturity and learning needs of students?

Moving into the next stage of schooling: A developmental perspective

Growth and development in children is characterised by sequential changes in their physical self, maturation, thinking, perception, skills and attitudes. These changes are also influenced heavily by their environment and the types of experiences children have been exposed to thus far in their lives.

By the age of 8 years old (Grade 3), they will have already begun to consolidate opinions, perspectives and attitudes about learning and school. They will be developing and holding a view about themselves, their self-esteem and confidence. Their feelings and beliefs about themselves as learners will become more defined. Empathic understanding is consolidating in their brain development, which means that they are looking at the world more broadly. Their awareness of the differences and similarities they have with others becomes quite pronounced. This is reflected in their forming of deeper levels of friendship and relationships. Their sense of values, morality, interests and identity will also now be forming more obviously, as will their sense of being accepted by their peers, and realising that each peer may have slightly or vastly different values, ideas, skills, family life or interests. They realise they are not quite as omnipotent as they thought they were in their early childhood years (when they often thought they were the most skilled and the best at everything!). Friendships—having a best friend or mate, increasingly trying to portray a sense of who they are as distinct from others, being with the 'in' crowd or the 'out' crowd—can become a big issue at this time.

Typical aspects of development and behaviour through these years include:

- wanting to voice opinions, to challenge authority, to gain a sense of ownership over their environment both at home and school

- accessing a range of technologies that expose them to a wider and sometimes inappropriate range of experiences

- starting to identify a preference with subjects that they describe as being 'good at', 'my favourite subject' or the areas of learning they don't like

- being more acutely aware of teachers and their personalities, behaviours and interactions with students.

Comments and conversations among students including things like, 'He is never fair', 'She is really a control freak' and 'He really gives you some choices and seems interested in us' are also quite common at this stage.

This stage of maturity sees significant shifts in brain development. Students are more able to construct understandings not only by engaging in concrete experiences but to varying degrees by representations in their mind, through abstract thinking, writing, speaking and listening, and through the use of other technologies.

Our understanding of the following changes in brain development associated with maturation during the middle and upper primary years informs our pedagogical perspective and thinking:

- development of empathic cognition

- symbolic representation

- friendships

- being ready to learn content

- self-esteem.

These changes require a slightly different emphasis in the teaching and learning strategies than those provided for students in the early years of primary school. It is important to note, however, that development and learning is influenced by a mix of each child's individual biological clock, genetic predispositions as well as environmental exposure and experiences. Educators must always be careful to pitch teaching and learning experiences to individual needs rather than relying on one-size-fits-all models or locking narrow sequences of maturation into specific chronological ages. This is particularly important as children are moving from Grade 2 into Grade 3. The developmental differences in maturity in these years is vast and the implications for pedagogy complex. There will be children who, despite being in the middle years of school, will still be within the early childhood spectrum developmentally. In this scenario, or where children are chronologically older but developmentally operating at a different maturity level, the WLA recommends a mix of the early years model (using investigations, see *Play Matters 2nd Edition*) running in parallel with the Grades 3–6 model.

Regardless of the stage of age and development, all children (and adults) learn most effectively when there is hands-on, real life exposure to learning opportunities that are as personalised as possible and relate in meaningful and engaging ways to each particular child and their interests.

Children develop best when they have secure, consistent relationships with responsive adults and opportunities for positive relationships with peers. Notably, positive teacher–child relationships promote children's learning and achievement, as well as social competence and emotional development.

Several prominent theories and bodies of research view cognitive development from the constructivist, interactive perspective (Naylor & Keogh 1999; Slavin 1990; Strike & Posner 1985). That is, young children construct their knowledge and understanding of the world in the course of their own experiences, as well as from teachers, family members, peers and older children, and from books and other media. They learn from the concrete (e.g., manipulatives); they also are capable of and interested in abstract ideas, to a far greater degree than was previously believed (Slavin 1990). Children take all this input and work out their own understandings and hypotheses about the world.

They try these out through interactions with adults and other children, physical manipulation, play and their own thought processes—observing what happens, reflecting on their findings, imagining possibilities, asking questions and formulating answers. When children make knowledge their own in these ways, their understanding is deeper and they can better transfer and apply their learning in new contexts (Copple & Bredekamp 2009).

Play, active investigation and project work are all important vehicles for developing self-regulation as well as for promoting language, cognition and social competence in children of all ages. Play gives children opportunities to develop physical competence and enjoyment of the outdoors, understand and make sense of their world, interact with others, express and control emotions, develop their symbolic and problem-solving abilities and practise emerging skills. Research shows strong links between play and foundational capacities such as memory, self-regulation, oral language abilities, social skills and success in school (Copple & Bredekamp 2009; Jones & Reynolds 1992).

Children's experiences shape their motivation and approaches to learning, such as persistence, initiative and flexibility; in turn, these dispositions and behaviours affect their learning and development. Development and learning advance when children are challenged to achieve at a level just beyond their current mastery, and also when they have many opportunities to practise newly acquired skills.

Developmentally appropriate practice: Preschool to the end of primary school

As discussed in detail in *Play Matters 2nd Edition*, developmentally appropriate practice (DAP) has been associated with early childhood and early years education all over the Western world since the 1950s (Copple & Bredekamp 2009). Aspects of DAP are used as the basis for the WLA and are relevant for teaching and learning across Grades 3–6.

DAP is based on the idea that children learn best from doing; when they are actively involved in their environment and build knowledge based on their experiences rather than through passively receiving information. Active learning environments promote hands-on learning experiences and allow children to interact with objects in their environment, as well as their peers and teachers.

DAP concepts include active learning experience, varied instructional strategies, and a balance between teacher-directed and child-directed activities. DAP informs the differentiation of teaching approaches for children's evolving stages of development. Figure 1.1 demonstrates this differentiation from preschool to lower primary and upper primary years. In the preschool setting, the focus is on play-based curriculum with intentional and responsive teaching,

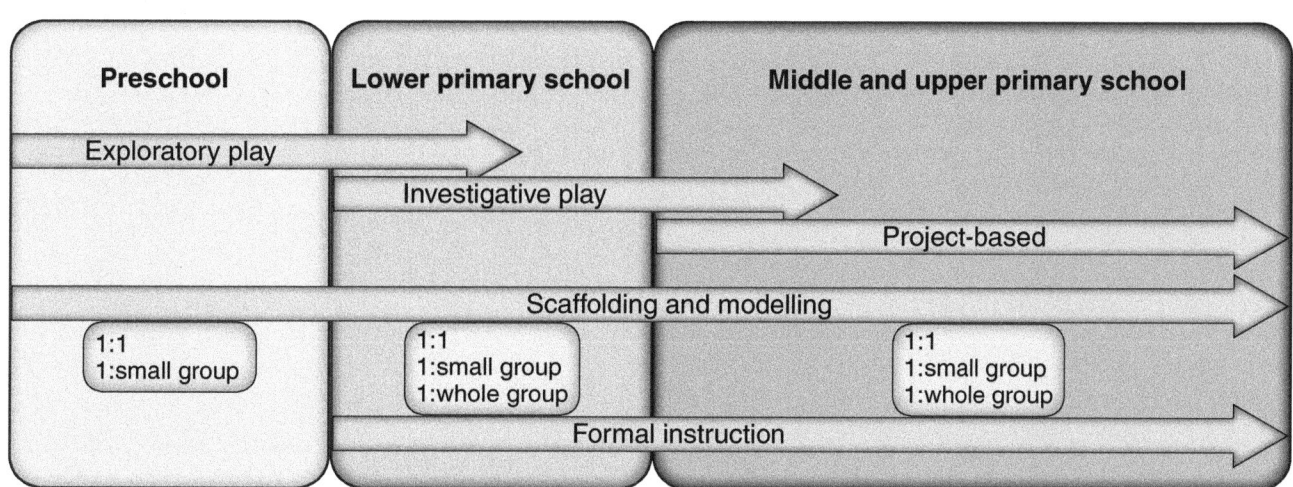

Figure 1.1 Developmentally appropriate practice informs the differentiation of teaching approaches that are appropriate for children's stage of development

1:1 or 1:small group with no formalised instruction. The lower years of primary school require concrete hands-on experiences balanced with intentional and responsive teaching, that is 1:1, 1:small group and formal instruction. In the middle and upper years of primary school, hands-on investigation takes the shape of projects with intentional and responsive teaching 1:1, 1:small group and formal instruction.

For an in-depth review of these concepts and how they are applied within the WLA framework, please see *Play Matters 2nd Edition*.

Defining the differences between curriculum, pedagogy, philosophy and values

Understanding the need for a whole-school philosophy is discussed in detail in *Play Matters 2nd Edition*, but as this is such a fundamental element of the WLA, it is worth considering these points again here. The WLA is an actual philosophy of teaching and learning that spans from preschool through to the lower, middle and upper primary years. It is not a curriculum or a teaching tool that is overlaid on an existing pedagogy, nor is it to be viewed as an 'add on' program that needs to be squeezed into the existing overcrowded timetable. The WLA is a pedagogy that underpins everything that happens in a day, a week and a year—and informs every moment of the teacher's intention to teach (planning, scaffolding, modelling, observing and directing). The philosophy and pedagogy of the WLA from preschool to Grade 6 is based on student empowerment, engagement and ownership alongside teacher direction, scaffolding and instruction.

As educators and researchers, we believe it is vital for schools to have clarity in key aspects of curriculum and philosophy to ensure that whatever major elements of teaching and learning are adopted within a school, there is consistency and transparency for teachers, parents and children. Schools wishing to implement the WLA require a clear understanding of what adopting a particular philosophy with associated teaching and learning strategies actually involves.

The terms pedagogy, philosophy, curriculum, program and values are often merged, used interchangeably, completely misrepresented or misunderstood. Table 1.1 provides a simple explanation of each of the terms to help school leaders and teachers clarify and purposefully plan their own school philosophy and pedagogy.

The importance of a whole-school philosophy

The exploration of any teaching and learning approach (and its subsequent implementation) requires school communities to clearly articulate the philosophy and practices to parents, teachers, children and others. Nothing can be more confusing and challenging for a school community than the fragmentation of practices and/or inconsistencies in approaches. Teachers, parents and children can become quite confused and lack confidence in what the school actually believes in if messages are inconsistent or unclear because there is no purposeful platform of philosophical understanding.

The more consistent and clearly articulated the overall philosophy and practices are within a school, the more effectively they can be introduced, supported and sustained. The results of many studies from across the world highlight the effectiveness and quality of teaching and learning when a consistent set of principles and practices are shared, understood and implemented rather than when individual teachers implement their own interpretations of curriculum requirements (Summers 1994; Weinstock, Starr & Fazzaro 1974; Wright, Horn & Sanders 1997). Many schools across Australia are now spending more time on internal professional development and meetings to work through what type of educational philosophy and associated pedagogy needs to be reflected across the whole school. At times this can be a challenging process. Some teachers may be resistant to change. Others may feel threatened or that the way they are teaching is being criticised.

In some education communities, the concept of an education philosophy is not well understood; this introduces complicating factors when trying to develop and embed a whole-school philosophy. For example,

- schools often have a mission or vision statement and a three-year strategic plan which are touted as the school's 'educational philosophy'

- terminology such as, 'to value individuals', 'to help every child succeed' or 'to build strong literacy and numeracy' are often mistakenly used as a philosophy. These statements are *values* that may be embedded within the philosophy but are not actually an educational philosophy that guides the practice of all staff working within that school

- teaching and learning tools are mistakenly used and thought of as an actual philosophy with associated key principles and practices. De Bono's six thinking hats is not a philosophy or pedagogy, nor is multiple intelligences. These are simply a range of interpretations of other theories that have been translated into particular tools for teaching alongside key principles of practice. Many schools which use the WLA would incorporate aspects of thinking hats or multiple intelligences simply as one part of a great whole in teaching and learning strategies.

Developing a whole-school philosophy

An educational philosophy is developed by following these well defined and purposeful steps and processes (see Figure 1.2):

1. Identify the key values the school community believes to be most relevant.

2. Match these values with theoretical underpinning.

Table 1.1 Terms and definitions to help leadership and teachers clarify and purposefully plan their own school philosophy and pedagogy

Term	Definition
Educational philosophy	A set of key beliefs based upon specific theoretical perspectives, research and values that underlie all practices in teaching and learning. An educational philosophy is not a framework designed by state or federal governments. A philosophy helps individual schools interpret and respond to government requirements and informs how teaching and learning will look.
Pedagogy	The 'how' of all teaching, learning, interactions and strategies which reflect and relate directly to the philosophy and are used consistently across a community.
Curriculum	Technically, curriculum refers to everything contained within an educational setting: the content, teaching, relationships, resources, environment and the 'how'. It is an overarching term. It is often mistakenly interpreted only as the content, outcomes or as a syllabus.
Program	This is a specific (often stand-alone) training unit such as a resiliency program, a restorative justice session or a social skills program.
Values	The underlying beliefs that a school places as a thread or context on which all teaching, learning and modelling are reflected. A value technically cannot be taught, but must be embedded within a school community.
Framework	Most frameworks provide an overview, outline or list of teaching and learning skills, knowledge and understandings that a state or federal government requires of schools. It rarely reflects a philosophy or pedagogy; most often it is a list of outcomes.
Outcomes/objectives	In recent years, education circles have adopted the term 'outcome' from economics. It refers to particular skills or knowledge that it is anticipated students will reach at particular times, years or grade levels. Outcomes can only be called outcomes once a student has achieved something. What are often labelled as 'outcomes' at the planning and framework stage should in fact be objectives, goals or intentions.
Tools	These are particular teaching activities that teachers use to help and support themselves and students in the teaching and learning process. Tools such as De Bono's thinking hats or Gardner's multiple intelligences for example are not educational philosophies or pedagogies; they are tools that can be used within particular philosophies, including the WLA.

3. Identify research that indicates the most effective teaching and learning strategies.

4. Identify educational philosophies and practices that best match the values of the school and the research that has highlighted best practice teaching and learning.

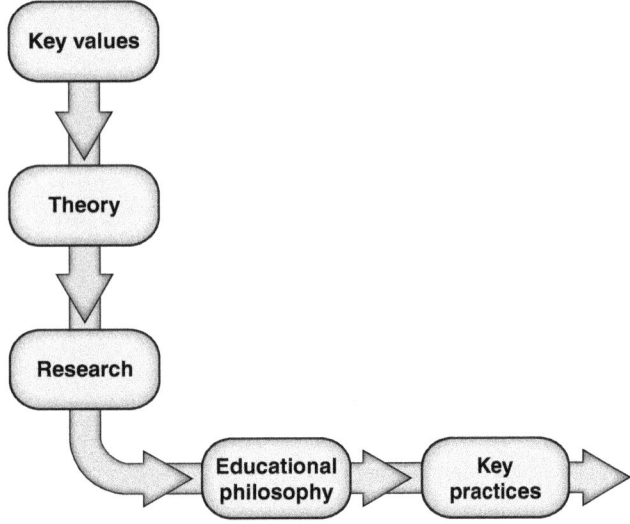

Figure 1.2 Process for the development of educational philosophy and practice

Note: Curriculum framework expectations are simply integrated within the existing philosophy and pedagogy.

An actual educational philosophy that has teaching strategies to match is an imperative for long-term effective teaching and learning within a school community. It is not appropriate or conducive for effective teaching and learning for each individual teacher or teaching team to implement their own style based simply on their past experiences or preferences. Few professions would accept separate practices within one professional community. This does not mean that all teachers are clones of each other and that there is no room for individualising learning environments that reflect the nature of the teacher and the students.

There is a significant difference between (i) a teacher just doing their own thing in their own room divorced of any deeply considered philosophy and research in education and (ii) a teacher making their own interpretation of the clarity set out in the school's philosophy.

Most schools that reflect strong leadership and commitment to a particular philosophy will also implement strategies to ensure the consistency of pedagogy continues even when leadership or staff move out of the school. This is demonstrated when schools advertise for staff that are aware of the key philosophy, principles and practices embedded within the school and have the skills and understanding to embrace this philosophy in their classrooms. Another example is when interview panels and questions are specifically determined to identify potential staff members who have an understanding of the particular philosophy and pedagogy of the school.

Strong and effective leadership will result in the core philosophy of the school being perpetuated even if there is a change in leadership. If a new principal is appointed in a school, the philosophy and pedagogy should not be changed overnight—this indicates that the appointment has been based on criteria which are not congruent with the most significant aspects of the school; that is the philosophy. A major factor of any appointment should be that the new principal embraces, understands and is committed to the philosophy of the school. This is one of the great challenges in mainstream education today. How does a school develop, sustain and implement a clear and consistent philosophy and pedagogy, and how is it maintained through staff and principal selection?

An educational philosophy directly informs how the teaching and learning will occur throughout the school community. Ideally, when implementing an educational philosophy such as the WLA, leadership and the school community have taken time to explore, understand, test and learn about the philosophy. The adoption of the approach, therefore, becomes an informed and well understood process that provides support to staff and information to parents and the wider community. This ensures not only successful implementation of the philosophy and successful learning for students, but a sustained and ongoing commitment to the philosophy that attracts likeminded teachers into the school. It also ensures leadership that has clarity and conviction of how the teaching and learning needs to look across the school or team. The important role of leadership is discussed in more detail in Chapter 3.

Summary

- Effective teaching and learning ideally requires a strong commitment to a shared philosophy and pedagogy that is consistent across a school.

- Teaching and learning must emphasise skills and 'learning how to learn', and not be preoccupied only with content and knowledge.

- Students require empowerment, ownership, engagement and motivation as key criteria in which to sustain learning and skills.

- Students require a mix of active investigation, research and some freedom to explore and construct learning based on their own interests alongside guidance, scaffolding, direction and instruction from their teachers.

- As students move into the middle and upper primary years, many aspects of their thinking and development are maturing and they require learning experiences and opportunities to match the specific needs and attributes across these years.

Chapter 2

The Walker Learning Approach Grades 3–6

'He who dares to teach must never cease to learn.'

Richard Henry Dann

Introduction

The Walker Learning Approach (WLA) was developed in the mid-1990s for the early years of schooling (see *Play Matters 2nd Edition*). It is now being implemented throughout Australia across the spectrum of schools including Catholic, Jewish, Islamic, independent and public schools. It is the true demonstration of authentic child-centred pedagogy; it doesn't matter who the child is, where they live, or what their culture or socioeconomic status is; this approach starts with considering where each individual is in their experience, learning and development.

This approach creates a seamless link between how children learn across their early childhood years and how they make a smoother and more effective transition as they move between preschool and school. It has succeeded in engaging children, particularly young boys, in their learning on a daily basis. It has a mix of formal instruction in literacy and numeracy alongside a strong emphasis upon engaging children through opportunities for personalised learning, self-expression, exploration and creativity which also integrates many aspects of literacy, numeracy, the arts, science and other key learning areas. In the early years, this is achieved through a mix of projects, investigations and directed play experiences. Empirical research shows that this approach leads to improved oral language, wellbeing, literacy and numeracy and engagement (particularly in boys) (Copple & Bredekamp 2009; Walker 2009).

The success of the approach in the early years has led to the development of the WLA (Grades 3–6), where the key principles of active, authentic and personalised engagement and learning can be continued into the middle and upper primary years. For these more mature children, a range of teaching and learning strategies are provided that still retain formal instruction alongside project-based learning experiences and other strategies designed to empower, engage and motivate learners. The extension of Walker Learning into the middle and upper years of primary ensures a seamless and consistent philosophy and pedagogy across all years of primary school.

Kathy Walker has worked with teachers since 2001 to develop and implement this approach into older cohorts without compromising the expectations and requirements of subjects, content and state and territory frameworks. This chapter provides a detailed description of the key elements of this approach for Grades 3–6 and how it works in a classroom and within a teaching team. It gives specific details on each main component of the approach and how they link to all areas of teaching and learning, including room set up, communication board, clinic groups, class meetings and education research projects (ERPs). Chapter 4 provides a more in-depth description and details of the ERP.

Key principles

The platform for the WLA embraces best pedagogical practice, developmentally appropriate practice and effective practical application. This is demonstrated below in the list of the principles that characterise the approach.

- Children's interests are used as part of the means for learning experiences alongside formal teaching of skills and understanding in literacy and numeracy.

- Children's interests are expanded, scaffolded and supported as a means of ongoing engagement in particular learning areas which relate to learning outcomes as determined by requirements of curriculum.

- Additional issues or concepts at a community or school level are incorporated within the planning document but not viewed or used as the 'topic' or 'theme' on which planning is based or all experiences are planned.

- Play- and project-based learning experiences are the major pedagogical tool for teaching and learning alongside formal instruction.

- The nature of experience promotes creativity, imagination and scope for children to invent and create and avoids cloned art work, large amounts of worksheets and stencils.

- Planning documentation identifies objectives for children's development in the first instance and in addition, identifies key learning intentions and children's interests as a basis for planning learning experiences which then link to learning intentions.

- Learning experiences emphasise active engagement and provide children with opportunities to explore the processes involved in learning and skill acquisition, not just end products. They seek to encourage children to pursue some of their learning experiences into ongoing projects for either short or longer periods of time.

- Observation and documentation by teachers of key skills, needs, strengths and interests of individual children is used to further plan and implement appropriate experiences and set further learning and developmental objectives.

- Skill instruction sessions (clinic groups) and small and large group times are still used within the classroom, including additional formal literacy and numeracy sessions each day.

- Teachers must still direct, scaffold, extend or intervene with children in order to ensure that children are actively engaged and learning.

- The notion of an 'integrated curriculum' within the WLA refers to all learning areas being recognised as integrated and embedded in children's learning and not discrete parts of the day where a particular content or focus area is taught with a topic.

- A balance is set by the teacher by what emerges from the child in response to the range of experiences provided by the teacher, and what the teacher wishes to introduce to the children in relation to skill and content.

- In practice, the WLA uses a mix of active hands-on project-based work, alongside group clinic times, personal reflection times, projects, skill instruction and other learning experiences provided by the school throughout the day.

The WLA draws upon elements of developmentally appropriate practice in order to ensure that well researched and longstanding principles of practice and implementation are maintained. In addition to incorporating some of the principles of developmentally appropriate practice, the WLA is also informed by empirical studies on teaching and learning from around the world—in particular two recent studies from the USA and UK which identify key criteria for effective, meaningful and sustained learning which produce high levels of engagement for students as they move into their middle and upper primary years (Alexander, Armstrong & Flutter et al. 2009; Miller & Almon 2009).

Key components

The WLA (Grades 3–6) reflects a system that continues to provide formal instruction and direction, and also reflect a set of additional strategies and practices for the teacher and students. Each component interconnects with the others to provide a holistic and consistent set of strategies in the teaching–learning cycle. To maintain the integrity and rigour of the approach, all the key components need to be working side by side. This is an important place to begin for understanding and working through the implementation. The WLA is a pedagogical philosophy that underpins intentional teaching across all aspects of teaching and learning throughout the day, week and year; it is not a simplistic addition of project-based learning overlaid on existing systems or tools. This understanding is very important as it conceptualises the platform for success in implementation, student engagement and consistent pedagogy.

The key components for the successful implementation of WLA are:

- creating an empowering and student-focused learning environment

- student–teacher–parent communication boards

- electronic media

- focus students

- clinic groups

- formal instruction teaching sessions

- student–teacher class meetings

- student project work (education research projects known as ERPs)
- expo
- teacher, self and peer assessment
- planning, documentation and reporting.

In the following sections, each component of the WLA is described in detail. The end of this chapter (p. 26) provides a more detailed description of the shape of days and weeks; however a synopsis of what the days and weeks look like is given below to help teachers understand each component in relation to the larger whole.

How does a day/week actually operate?

Each week features nine major aspects to the teaching and learning cycle.

1. Formal instruction in literacy, numeracy and other subject areas. This is reflected by a number of strategies including:
   - whole group instruction
   - clinic group instruction
   - modelling
   - project expectations and requirements
   - 1:1 work between student and teacher.
2. Project-based learning (ERP).
3. Clinic groups.
4. Class meeting.
5. Student journal/diary.
6. Specialist or other programs provided by the school.
7. Communication board.
8. Focus students.
9. Assessment.

The descriptions and examples provided here are for a 'regular classroom' of one teacher in one class. However, schools using the WLA reflect a wide range of different physical spaces and learning environments, including team teaching, whole area teaching, multi-age and rural classrooms with all grades together. Despite these different learning environments, the fundamental principles and strategies are the same. Be reassured that no classroom is too small or space too large for this approach to be implemented successfully.

Creating an empowering and student-focused learning environment

During the 1990s there was an emphasis on group work and children sitting together with the intention of producing students who could 'cooperate'. This is ironic given that many perspectives indicate that a slightly different approach is required to provide a learning environment that best supports the individual with concentration, independence and interdependence, and for students to be engaged and empowered (Fisher 2006). Furthermore, there is evidence demonstrating that students are often disengaged and dislike having to work for the majority of each day in 'cooperative groups' (Edith Cowan University 2008).

Successful learning and meaningful engagement requires everyone (children and adults) to be able to work both independently and interdependently. Most students spend at least 6 hours every day having to share space, resources, a teacher, time with each other and are almost constantly interacting at various levels with others. The WLA places an emphasis on students having some personal space as well as a collective space and place within the learning environment.

We recognise that by the time students reach Grades 3 and 4 (and particularly Grades 5 and 6) they are developing a greater and deeper sense of identity. They need and have a right to feel that their learning environment reflects something about who they are, and that it provides opportunities for contributing ideas, reflecting upon their own learning, needs and strengths, taking some responsibilities for their own learning and environment, and communicating in a broad range of mediums.

When Grade 5 or 6 students are asked, 'How would you like your learning environment to look?', they frequently respond with: 'We want old fashioned desks so we can have our own space, we want to be able to work together just sometimes and we want a communal area with a couch and table to sit and talk with our friends.' The philosophy underpinning the WLA requires the 'de-institutionalisation' of the regular classroom where there are rows or circles of bare tables all the same colour, all at the same height with very few additional resources, experiences or furnishings (certainly not designed to set up engagement or motivation).

The learning environment is described as the 'third teacher' by many theorists and approaches from across the world (Edwards, Gandini & Forman 1998; Pairman & Terreni 2001). The learning environment for children in these middle and upper years of primary education requires surroundings that match their stage of development, provide stimulation and opportunities for exploration, engagement, empowerment and excitement simply by the way they are set up and how much students are encouraged to contribute to and establish the space. Just re-arranging the table settings each term is not particularly engaging for students. A stimulating physical space in itself can provide learning opportunities, engagement and exposure to a variety of different and additional experiences. It also creates a strong sense of identity, empowerment and creates a culture of inclusiveness and stimulation. The WLA environment is best represented by:

- individual small tables (these can be brought together at times, but respect the independence and personal space of each child). Some tables may be higher (to invite different modes of working), such as an art room or trestle table

- a sofa area that is relaxed, perhaps with a coffee table, magazines, books

- some semi-enclosed or divided areas so the environment feels more cosy and less sterile (some schools use curtains hung from the ceiling, others use trellis or bookshelves)

- tables do not dominate the space and are not all in the middle of the room or around the edge of the room

- lighting is soft at times, trying to avoid fluorescent lights for the entire day

- rich with print, posters and text but not so much that it is over-stimulating

- the use of neutral colours and ideally natural materials such as wood rather than plastic for furniture, props, walls, etc. so that the children themselves create the richness

- well organised space that is not messy or too cluttered. Disorganised spaces lead to messy, disorganised behaviour and learning.

- access to outside spaces ideally, or areas not confined only to the classroom

- if space permits, a few small work centres such as a technology/electronic station with cameras, videos, computers, software programs such as animation; a resource centre with paper, clipboard, pens, tape measures, materials for constructing; a construction area of Lego Technic; a media centre; a music centre

- tubs or shelves of equipment that students have freedom to access when appropriate such as clay, wire, cardboard, natural materials, microscopes, etc. in order to promote a range of mediums.

The idea is to ensure that the learning environment has a feel about it that reflects the specific individuals and class each year. This naturally changes and modifies itself depending upon the students and the teacher. In addition, it aims to promote a more engaging atmosphere and a greater sense of ownership and identity for the students.

Student–teacher–parent communication boards

Four essential and integral aspects of the WLA are to empower students to take some responsibility for their own learning, to identify some of their own learning needs, to practise being organised, and to be able to communicate through a variety of methods about their learning and interests. The student–teacher–parent communication board is one of the methods used to develop these skills.

The communication board is a hands-on, easily accessible board that provides information on a daily, weekly, and term basis. It is shared in terms of responsibility between students and teachers; it is open, communicative and inviting.

Establishing and setting up the communication board

The communication board is a pin board in order to easily post and change information.

It must be:

- at student height for reading and reaching
- separate from other whiteboards and noticeboards
- uncluttered, very organised, categorised and neat
- easily viewed or accessed by parents
- large enough to contain and display key documents.

Key documents include:

- the fortnightly statement of intent (displayed at A3 size)
- term overview of key learning intentions
- general timetable for the week
- proposed agenda for class meeting (with opportunities for students to add to this)
- key term incursions/excursions
- clinic group section:
  - ideas posted by students for the types of clinic groups they might like
  - section for offering to run a clinic or suggestions of someone who may be invited to conduct a clinic group
  - compulsory clinic group listing each day or week
  - optional clinic group listing each day or week
- a section for student comments, additional ideas, thoughts, issues
- any other sections that staff or students may wish to add. Examples include a graffiti section, an affirmation section or a photo gallery.

How and when to establish the communication board

The communication board needs to be up and running as soon as a teacher or team are to commence implementation of the WLA. The aims and purposes of the approach are immediately compromised without the opportunities for students to self-select, to take responsibility for their learning each day and to check in with the board.

Depending on the teacher and the group, there are a number of ways that the board can be instigated and established. Remember that part of the aim of the board is to empower and create a sense of ownership and pride in the students' learning environment and in learning itself. The teacher may provide the key criteria/sections the board must have and allow the students to design, discuss and organise the board, or the teacher may establish the board in the first instance but over time may encourage students to add, decorate or input ideas to improve and update the board.

How do students use the communication board?

The aim is for each student to develop a pattern and expectation that the learning day commences with 'checking in' on the board before anything else happens. There is a range of ways in which this process can be organised.

- The board is in an area where the students congregate before school commences. In this way, they are not all trying to access the board at exactly the same time.
- Students are provided with a few additional minutes on arrival to check the board and write any clinic groups or other information

they need for the day in their journal or laptop. This is viewed as part of their learning (taking responsibility), not as a waste of teaching time.

- A teacher's assistant (student from the class) is assigned on a weekly basis to update the board each week or each day. This role is an important one and is shared across all students of the class on a roster system.

- Students can access, update and check the board throughout each day.

Electronic media

The integration and use of electronic tools and resources is an important part of any teaching and learning environment. The WLA values the use of electronic or technology-based experiences as tools rather than as separate activities. Often the use of computers and other technologies becomes artificial or an excuse to opt out of deep learning investigations and research, and involves simply cutting and pasting slabs of information or playing computer games.

A major aim of the WLA is to empower students to take responsibility for much of their own organisation and learning. The use of electronic and technological means for organisation planning, researching and timetabling as well as for some modes of communication are all part of the approach.

Examples and ideas include:

- students using netbooks or electronic organisers to add to their daily timetable

- using the Ultranet for students and teachers to post notes or updates of information in addition to and alongside the noticeboard

- students using emails and uploading photographs of their learning

- use of video cameras (such as Flip cameras) for documenting/scripting/reporting

- Skype sessions

- software programs such as claymation for projects

- technologies can also be used for project work (ERPs).

The WLA avoids the use of computer labs as separate and discrete sessions, although the approach accommodates the need for introducing students to specific skills.

Focus students

On at least four days each week, 2 or 3 children are 'focus students'. The aim is to have all students in the class to be a focus student once per fortnight. Focus students are rostered so that teachers, students and parents are aware of who will be a focus student each day. The roster is displayed on the communication board.

Key aims and roles of focus students

- Each focus student shares with the class for a few minutes at the commencement and the end of the day. The students share something about their learning, ERP, what aspects or interests they currently have and some of their personal learning goals.

- The group are invited to ask questions, contribute ideas and support.

- The group are also provided with information about the actual ERP each student is working on.

- During the day, the teacher spends a few minutes with each of the focus students individually for what is called 'student-led conferencing'. This is where each focus student—at their own direction—shares with the teacher some of their feelings, work, skills or details of their ERP project. Student-led conferencing with each focus child aims not only to personalise learning but also to build and extend a meaningful and positive relationship with each student on a regular basis.

Clinic groups

The philosophy of the WLA includes creating an environment where students view learning and teaching as:

Chapter 2 The Walker Learning Approach Grades 3–6

- a process that incorporates learning and skills shared and delivered not only by a teacher but by students, parents and other members of the community

- a process whereby students are encouraged to identify areas of skill and knowledge where they believe they need more support or practice in or wish to share with others

- opportunities for students to share their own expertise, skills, talents and interests

- opportunities to participate in small group learning where a particular skill or interest is shared and learned together

- an inclusive situation where time and opportunities are provided for students to offer suggestions for learning

- a process that involves students self-directing, reflecting and identifying their own needs or strengths

- opportunities to opt in to specific clinic teaching sessions that will support a particular skill that is required.

Clinic groups create opportunities to include all these aspects into the teaching and learning environment. They are small group learning experiences where teachers and others can scaffold, revise, extend and support students in focusing on a specific skill or interest. Some clinic groups are based upon student interests; some are based on literacy and numeracy instruction; some are based on other specific skills or concepts the teacher requires the students to learn. Some clinic groups are compulsory (as set by the teacher) and others are optional. The aim is for the clinic groups to be conducted by a variety of people such as teachers, students, other staff, parents and community members.

Clinic groups:

- are a range of different small group learning situations (in content, presentation style and skills)

- are pre-planned and organised each week through discussion and the communication board (which is updated at least each Monday morning before students arrive)

- can occur at any time during a school day or after hours if appropriate. Often one clinic group will be conducted during ERP time. This can be on any focus, not necessarily just on the ERP issues

- provide time and opportunity to personalise learning

- provide opportunities to gather in small groups where relationship building is facilitated and developed between students and staff or students and other leaders

- will often be led by the classroom teacher, but leaders will also include students from the class or school, other teachers, the principal, community members, friends and/or family

- reflect a range of different aspects of life and learning

- may include literacy, numeracy, hobbies or interests and be knowledge- or skills-based.

Clinic group aims

- to promote greater levels of self responsibility and student reflection on specific skills in any subject area they may need practice in, additional support or extension with, but particularly literacy and numeracy

- to provide more personalised learning experiences throughout each day

- to provide the opportunity for students to practise self assessment and to identify their needs and strengths

- to empower students to select, suggest or run a clinic group to support self or others

- to contribute to, organise and support the communication board notices and ideas

- for students to participate in the teaching and learning process by conducting some clinic groups if and where appropriate

- for students to see teaching and learning in a wider perspective than just the teacher teaching, including having other staff, students, community members or parents conducting clinic groups.

Clinic groups are conducted at any time of day. Usually one is conducted during ERP time (about 10–15 minutes) and may be related to a skill that is relevant to ERPs (for example, how to present a graphic organiser, or how to represent data from an ERP in a range of ways using IT skills).

The approach provides the opportunity for students each week to have a combination of whole-group sessions with teachers, and clinic groups that are a mix of compulsory and opt-in options. Students are encouraged to identify particular clinic groups they think they might need.

Clinic group examples

Clinic groups over a period of a month would generally include:

- literacy groups—particular skills in any areas of literacy (usually every day)
- numeracy groups—particular skills in any areas of numeracy (usually every day)
- interest groups—there may be a particular interest, hobby or skill that a parent, student or teacher may wish to share (usually twice a week minimum)
- organisation skill group—this may be how to write a timeline, present a graphic organiser, write a plan, organise personal work or desk (usually twice a week minimum)
- other subject group—this may be an additional session on communication, graphic design, history, science, etc. (usually once a week minimum)
- ERP group—this may focus on a particular project of a student or a range of issues the teacher wants to add information to for particular students (usually once or twice a week, or during ERP sessions)
- skill group—this may include any other specific skills, life skills or learning skills that may be of interest or required (usually once or twice a week)
- optional student-led group—at any time during a week that suits teachers and students.

How do clinic groups work?

Consistent with any teaching and learning, teachers predetermine specific skills and needs of students as well as particular new skills and concepts they wish to introduce or practise as a focus. Some skills are relevant to some students at various times more than others; students with similar skills, needs or mixed abilities can be organised into clinic groups for further scaffolding and extension. (See p. 23 for examples.)

What are other students doing during a clinic group?

Quite simply, what they would usually be doing while a teacher works with small groups: independent learning, project work, additional literacy or numeracy work.

Compulsory clinic groups

These are predetermined by the teacher. Lists of the students required are posted either weekly or daily on the communication board. Students are expected to check the communication board each day to identify if they are expected at a clinic group at any specific time or times. During each morning 'tuning in' session, students are reminded or prompted to check the communication board. This is designed to facilitate independence and self responsibility. There are usually a few places left in the clinic group for other students to enter their name if they feel they need or may benefit from attending. This can still be at the teacher's discretion, but the process encourages students to self-select and identify their own needs or interests.

Optional clinic groups (opt-in/self-select)

Optional clinic groups provide opportunities for students to self-select into these clinics and choose particular clinic groups of interest or skill. These clinic groups are posted in the same manner as compulsory clinics (daily or weekly) and still capped to ensure small group, personalised scaffolding and interactions.

Formal instruction teaching sessions

Many educators misunderstand or misinterpret approaches to teaching and learning that emphasise active investigation and project-based work such as the WLA. They mistakenly assume that active engagement and a broader range of choice in some aspects of teaching and learning equates with a lack of intention or a lack of formal instruction. There will always be experiences and learning sessions where there may be little or no choice for students and it is compulsory for all students to participate.

The WLA draws heavily from international research which recognises that children require a mix of formal instruction as well as some choices (even though the choices are carefully guided and scaffolded by the teacher) (Goeke 2008). Throughout a day or week, there will be a range of different learning opportunities for the students, and many of these will include specific and formal instruction.

Within the week there may be:

- whole group tuning in at commencement of each day
- whole group reflection at the end of each day
- whole group overview or revision, or a new teaching session on a specific literacy, numeracy or other subject skill
- clinic groups (compulsory and optional; formal and informal teaching)
- literacy/reading sessions
- writing sessions
- numeracy sessions
- specialist programs
- ERPs.

All teaching and learning within the WLA is intentional and planned, and learning goals are always shared with students and pre-planned by teachers. Some sessions will be formal and instructional; some will include modelling; some will be with the whole group and other times will be in clinic groups. The major point is that there is nothing actually free or unplanned, and no subject or skill that is overlooked or avoided.

Planning is still required both in relation to state/territory and national frameworks, term goals and intentions, fortnightly intentions and individual plans (refer to Chapter 5 for planning). The WLA introduces a much deeper and broader range of skills and concepts into the learning environment, while still covering specific skills, concepts and content as required.

Student–teacher class meetings

Many learning environments recognise the importance of empowering students to voice and share their opinions, feelings, experiences and ideas as part of their own learning and development and as part of what it means to belong to, contribute to and function within a community.

The WLA includes a weekly class meeting. This meeting includes an agenda with some specific aims and criteria in order to ensure respectful and useful interactions as well as appropriate responses and actions that may result.

Aims of the class meeting

Class meetings provide:

- opportunities for shared conversations among a whole group
- a model of the importance of collective community sharing and coming together
- encouragement of interactions within a group broader than the smaller sub-groups, clinic groups or friendship groups students usually share with
- practice in expressing opinions or views about a range of issues, including global issues,

Examples of compulsory clinic groups

Compulsory Clinic Group

Revision of decimal point operations
Monday 12th July 10.00 am (during numeracy session)
Conducted by: Teacher's name
Description: Revision of decimal point placement when multiplying numbers with decimal places
Maximum participants: 6
Student's name: (entered by teacher)
Student's name: (entered by teacher)
Student's name: (entered by teacher)
Student's name: (entered by teacher)
Student's name: (entered by student)
Student's name: (entered by student)

Compulsory Clinic Group

Building a graphic organiser
Tuesday 13th July 2.00 pm (during ERP time)
Conducted by: Principal's name
Description: This is the second clinic group, building on the introduction session held on Tuesday 6th July, and will practise using a Lotus diagram
Maximum participants: 5
Student's name: (entered by teacher)
Student's name: (entered by teacher)
Student's name: (entered by teacher)
Student's name: (entered by student)
Student's name: (entered by student)

Examples of optional clinic groups

Optional Clinic Group

Digital photography and videoing/animation
Monday 12th July 1:00 pm (during ERP time)
Conducted by: Name of IT support person
Description: This is the first of a series of 4 clinic groups; during these sessions students will learn how to upload videos, edit videos and incorporate digital photos into a variety of projects
Maximum participants: 4
Student's name: (entered by teacher)
Student's name: (entered by teacher)
Student's name: (entered by student)
Student's name: (entered by student)

Optional Clinic Group

Pie graph design using computers
Tuesday 13th July 11:00 am (during numeracy session)
Conducted by: Student's mother (who teaches maths at a university)
Description: [Student's mother] will demonstrate how data can be manipulated on the computer to generate pie charts (editing of labelling, colours, shapes, 3D and images)
Maximum participants: 6
Student's name: (entered by teacher)
Student's name: (entered by teacher)
Student's name: (entered by teacher)
Student's name: (entered by teacher)
Student's name: (entered by student)
Student's name: (entered by student)

school issues and classroom issues and interactions

- opportunities to share ideas or future directions for learning

- practice in reflection, consideration, planning and negotiating.

The class meeting is not designed to be a gripe or restorative justice-type session, or viewed as a session for raising behaviours or issues that are not desirable. The WLA philosophy recommends that significant issues related to social interactions, behaviours and inappropriate actions between specific students are most effectively resolved or dealt with in private and respectful dialogue between the students involved and facilitated by a teacher/adult rather than a whole-group session.

How to conduct the weekly class meeting

- Establish a time of the week which is regular, respected and not changed regularly.

- Assign a student to lead and chair the meeting each week (post this on the communication board each Monday).

- The teacher will have a preliminary chat with the student chair before the meeting for scaffolding, suggestions, directions by the teacher and contributions and ideas by the student (topics of discussion could include World Cup soccer, elections, current issues in media, responses or opinions about a global, community or school issue).

- Students will have had an opportunity to raise and list issues for discussion at the weekly meeting on the communication board.

- The suggested agenda and issues to be discussed is prepared (see Figure 2.1). This can be distributed in paper form; listed on the communication board or whiteboard or simply verbally presented (it may include photos or newspaper items through an interactive whiteboard). Students are encouraged to add items to the agenda depending on how many topics are already listed.

- The student chair opens the meeting, asking someone to take notes of anything worth noting (a laptop is recommended) and leads the discussion with some of the agenda item issues. For example,

  - 'Our first issue today is the school performance and our role in it.'

  - 'Our first issue today is what we think of the federal election campaign.'

  - 'Are there any issues that anyone would like to raise today about how our classroom is operating?'

  - 'We have a choice for next term of whether our ERPs will be based on the subject focus of history or health. What do we think we want?'

- The student chair and teacher ensure students are encouraged to speak, to share and not to dominate or avoid.

- Each person is given the opportunity to speak and not be interrupted for about 3 minutes. The teacher may need to model this in the first instance.

- General interactive social rules apply, such as expressing opinions but not denigrating or criticising anyone at a personal level.

- The meeting lasts for approximately 20 or 30 minutes.

- A list of the major issues discussed, any action or goals set or any other aspects that need to be recorded are listed and compiled in a class meeting journal.

- The meeting journal is used from time to time to reflect, discuss, evaluate and inform.

- The journal is available for parents to view and read for information sharing.

- There is no secret business or hidden agendas in this process.

Education research projects

The education research project (ERP) is a major and integral aspect of the WLA. ERPs are much more than project-based learning and require great clarity from the teaching team. The ERP is a significant aspect of the teaching and learning of particular subject requirements and outcomes, including literacy and numeracy. It replaces the traditional Integrated Studies Topic of Inquiry but continues to address key content, concepts and skills required through various state, territory and federal frameworks.

The ERP is one of the most unique features of the WLA and teachers will need to spend considerable time unpacking and implementing the concept. A separate chapter has been dedicated to the depth of understanding required to implement the ERP with integrity and rigour. See Chapter 4 for all details and information as well as the Appendices or CD for templates and examples.

Expo

A wonderful feature of the WLA is the expo which is held each term. It is an opportunity for students to share with others—both within and outside the school community—some aspects of their learning, particularly their ERPs.

The emphasis of the expo is not a 'show and tell' of each finished project, but rather an in-depth opportunity for students to speak about and share aspects of their interests, the skills they are developing and the proposal process.

Details of how the expo is conducted including the students' role in planning, preparing and running the expo are included in the ERP chapter.

Planning, documentation and reporting

The planning process is described in detail in Chapter 5. Planning includes not only state/federal framework outcomes but term and fortnightly planning to ensure dynamic and responsive teaching and learning.

Planning is not so prescriptive that teachers are not able to adapt, respond or modify teaching and learning to meet the needs and interests of the children at any specific time, but it ensures that intention, proactive direction, learning experiences, clinic groups, whole group and formal instruction sessions are proactively

---

Class Meeting Agenda
Week 1, February 2011

The class meeting will be held this week on Friday afternoon. Please add any issues you would like raised. Our main focus will be on world events.

Leader: Kathy

Note-taker: Shona

Agenda items for discussion

- What happened across the world during the school summer break? (This was placed by teacher to give students the idea and start a discussion.)
- What issues are around in our local community or school at the current time?
- The Australian Open Tennis (student suggestion)
- The classroom table arrangements (student suggestion)

Figure 2.1 Example class meeting agenda

planned and implemented appropriately and responsively.

Planning includes both whole-group and individual planning processes and also provides opportunities for students to add to the planning.

Teacher, self and peer assessment

The WLA places an emphasis on authentic assessment and does not assume that all students are ready and able to reach the same outcomes at the same time or in the same way. The WLA reflects international research that highlights the importance of self assessment, peer assessment and assessment that is collected over time, and builds on and informs future planning, teaching and learning (Black & Wiliam 1998).

The WLA recognises that standardised testing and other government requirements and regulations necessitate a specific set of assessment and testing tools. However, the WLA provides a refreshing, richer and deeper set of assessment and reporting strategies which can add value, depth and meaning to students, teachers and parents. Chapter 6 explains the range of assessment, reporting, sharing and reflection of learning that is recommended.

How a day and week looks and operates

The ways that the weeks and days link together to promote a seamless and smooth continuity are a significant part of the integrity of the WLA. It is important that links to learning are made explicitly by the teacher at various parts of the day in the full range of different teaching and learning components. Table 2.1 demonstrates a typical weekly timetable.

The WLA seeks to promote authentic engagement that supports and encourages students to see the relevance of literacy and numeracy that can link back into ERPs and other aspects of their life and

Table 2.1   Example of a typical weekly timetable

	Weekly Timetable				
	Monday	**Tuesday**	**Wednesday**	**Thursday**	**Friday**
9.00 am	Tuning in Literacy session	Tuning in Library	Tuning in ERP	Tuning in Numeracy session	Tuning in Class meeting
10.00 am	Literacy session Clinic group	Library	ERP Clinic group	Numeracy session Clinic group	Specialist
11.00 am	Recess				
11.30 am	Numeracy session Clinic group	Sport	Literacy session	ERP	Literacy session Clinic group
1.00 pm	Lunch				
1.40 pm	ERP	Literacy session Clinic group	Literacy session Clinic group	Art	Numeracy session Clinic group
2.30 pm	ERP	ERP Clinic group	Numeracy session	Art	Specialist
3.10 pm	Reflection	Reflection	Reflection	Reflection	Reflection

learning. The aim is to ensure that students do not view their literacy, numeracy, clinic groups or ERPs as being totally separate from each other or that there are no links between each subject. In this sense the WLA is a truly integrated teaching and learning approach, even though we do encourage separate times for clinic groups, ERPs, literacy and numeracy.

A typical day in the Walker Learning classroom

The start of the day (each morning)

The assigned teacher's assistant (student) ensures they arrive in time to meet with the teacher in order to update the communication board ready for students to check in and organise their day. The day and weekly timetable as well as key learning intentions will also be listed.

The first ten minutes of the morning—before the formal commencement of the day—can be allocated to students for checking in. This checking in stage is an important part of students taking responsibility for their own learning and daily organisation. This time must be viewed by teachers, parents and students as part of the learning process and not rushed or overlooked because 'more important' things have to happen.

When students arrive, they check in at the communication board and note what clinic groups they may wish to 'opt in to' for the day. They may note their particular duties, jobs or clinic groups they must attend. They have time to read other notices or updates from teacher or students. Once checking stage is complete the class moves into 'tuning in'.

Tuning in (approximately 20 minutes)

Tuning in for WLA (Grades 3–6) uses the same philosophy as the tuning in that is implemented in the WLA across the first three years of school. Tuning in includes preparing, reflecting, organising, planning and scaffolding learning for the whole day. In addition, to accommodate the greater maturity and cognitive development of the students in Grades 3–6, the tuning in takes a slightly different shape and purpose. Table 2.2 provides a breakdown of the major components of tuning in.

Table 2.2 The core elements of a tuning-in session

	Tuning in
Approximately 5 minutes	Welcome Overview of the day Check communication board Diary entries General issues
Approximately 5 minutes	Clarifying learning intentions Quick review/revisit of current learning in literacy, numeracy, other subject areas
Approximately 10 minutes	Focus students General discussion: • ERP • Other learning • Other issues
	Dispersal into next part of the day

There are four major parts to tuning in:

1. Teacher gives a general welcome and ensures all students have checked in with the communication board and updated their diaries. Teacher reinforces the key parts to the day, when clinic groups will be operating, etc. An opportunity for general questions about the day is provided to the students.

2. An overview and reminder or quick revision of what key learning is being focused on at the present time, including key literacy, numeracy, other subject areas.

3. Focus students share aspects of their learning and ERPs that they are currently working on with peers.

4. Students then move into learning, specialist sessions or clinics.

Remainder of the day

This is completely up to the individual teacher or team and school timetable.

- Students may commence an ERP session where the teacher will work with focus students or others in student-led conferencing. Conducting an ERP session is described in detail in Chapter 4 and case studies are presented in Chapter 7.

- Students may participate in a whole group instruction session in literacy or numeracy and then move into independent literacy/numeracy work while the teacher conducts a clinic group.

- Students may be involved in specialist programs or other programs within the school.

- Students may be involved in independent work or attending clinic groups being offered across the unit or school.

- Students may be in clinic groups, independent reading or other learning as directed by teacher.

Reflection (at the end of each day)

This is an important part of the day. The teacher and students reflect for about 15–20 minutes on the learning that has occurred during the day and any issues that arose. They also make plans for the next day or week. The teacher reminds students about checking in for the following morning with the communication board. The focus students briefly report back on their own learning during the day and share with students who are encouraged to ask questions or make comments or suggestions.

Reflection time may involve use of photos, discussions, sharing of work or learning in a variety of ways. Table 2.3 provides a breakdown of the major components of reflection.

Table 2.3 The core elements of a reflection session

Reflection	
Approximately 5 minutes	General summary of the day's learning
Approximately 5–10 minutes	Focus students will reflect
Approximately 5–10 minutes	Organise and prepare for the next day Communication board Remind focus students for next day

Across a week

Each week, the learning environment continues to provide a range of key teaching and learning strategies. These include:

- literacy and numeracy sessions (these may be whole-group, clinic groups or independent work)

- ERP sessions (these are held at least 3 or 4 times each week, and link most directly to other subject outcomes such as history, society and environment, health)

- specialist teachers and other programs

- clinic groups

- student-led conferencing with focus students (each day)

- class meeting (once a week)

- tuning in (each morning or at the beginning of the ERP session)

- reflection (each afternoon or at the conclusion of the ERP session).

Note: It is important that focus students are scheduled each day. Even if there is not an ERP session, focus students can discuss, share and reflect on their learning re: ERPs during tuning in and reflection.

The WLA is a holistic approach to teaching and learning. It requires a number of key elements that fit together and link across different subject requirements and learning intentions to provide a greater continuity for students and to build a set of life skills necessary for effective and sustained learning and empowerment. The WLA is not just an ERP.

Summary

The WLA has at its core the key principles of active, authentic and personalised engagement and learning. The program for Grades 3–6 builds on the practices and principles of the WLA being implemented from preschool to Grade 2 and provides developmentally appropriate practice for students in the middle and upper years of primary.

- Learning experiences emphasise active engagement and provide children with opportunities to explore the processes involved in learning and skill acquisition, not just end products. They seek to encourage children to pursue some of their learning experiences as ongoing projects for either short or longer periods of time.

- Skill instruction sessions (clinic groups) and small and large group times are still used within the classroom, including additional formal literacy and numeracy sessions each day.

- Teachers must still direct, scaffold, extend or intervene with children in order to ensure that children are actively engaged and learning.

- A subject-based focus applies for each term, related to outcomes from state/national frameworks rather than topics of inquiry.

The key components for the successful implementation of WLA are:

- creating an empowering and student-focused learning environment

- student–teacher–parent communication boards

- electronic media

- focus students

- clinic groups (compulsory and optional)

- formal instruction teaching sessions

- student–teacher class meetings

- student project work (ERPs)

- expo

- teacher, self and peer assessment

- planning, documentation and reporting.

Chapter 3

Recommendations for schools introducing the Walker Learning Approach

'It takes courage to play in a world that does not play.'

Fred Donaldson

Introduction

Through our experiences over the past 17 years, we have witnessed a whole spectrum of effective and sustained implementations of the WLA. In this chapter we present a synthesis of international research identifying the key elements of a successful execution of any new pedagogy, along with our own experiences working with leadership teams and teachers as they embrace the WLA philosophy to teaching and learning. Especially important are the processes that help professionals transition through change in the workplace.

In Chapters 1 and 2 we have described and unpacked how the WLA actually works in Grades 3–6 and the key elements contained within the approach. In this chapter we want to encourage the reader to carefully consider and understand the importance of the following suggestions and recommendations to avoid as many challenges and difficulties as possible. This will provide the opportunity for the school to enjoy the process of exploring and implementing the approach as well as to ensure that the integrity, quality and rigour of the approach are upheld.

Successful implementation of a teaching and learning philosophy

We strongly recommend the following elements are considered when a school community wishes to embark on implementing the Walker Learning Approach.

Leadership is everything

It may sound like stating the obvious, but leadership in education (particularly in education communities such as schools) is one of the most important, influential and empowering roles. Without strong, clear and visionary leadership, a school community almost always eventually lacks clarity of vision and philosophy and as a result lacks consistent practices.

Leadership is different from management. The role of leadership is to articulate the vision for the school and to set clear goals that help the community move from the current perspective to future intentions. The leader must 'lead'; that is, they must develop a strategic plan that clearly articulates objectives, goals, action tasks and timelines that are consistent with the direction, philosophy and pedagogy of the community (see Figure 3.1).

It is often commented on—and we would agree—that the leaders within a school community best able to implement a whole-school philosophy such as the WLA are those who have expertise with and an understanding of philosophy and pedagogy. The importance of these qualities is often underestimated, resulting in other staff with a lesser understanding of pedagogy, whole-school philosophy and research about teaching and learning being assigned roles that are outside the scope of their expertise (for example, curriculum coordinators or professional development coordinators). Often a whole-school approach is not even on the radar, rather professional development budgets are provided to individuals or teams that may all be doing things completely separately, in ignorance of and often in opposition to each other!

Recommendations for leadership

Some of the most effective implementations of pedagogical philosophies we have witnessed in schools which adopt and use the WLA, have happened when the principal and leadership team ensure the following:

- They have a full knowledge and understanding of the approach.

- In dialogue with teaching staff, they set the agenda and future direction of teaching and learning in the school.

- They ensure that parents and the entire school community are aware of and have some understanding of the direction and commitment of the school's teaching and learning.

- They allocate time, funding and resources in order to support staff throughout the implementation of the approach.

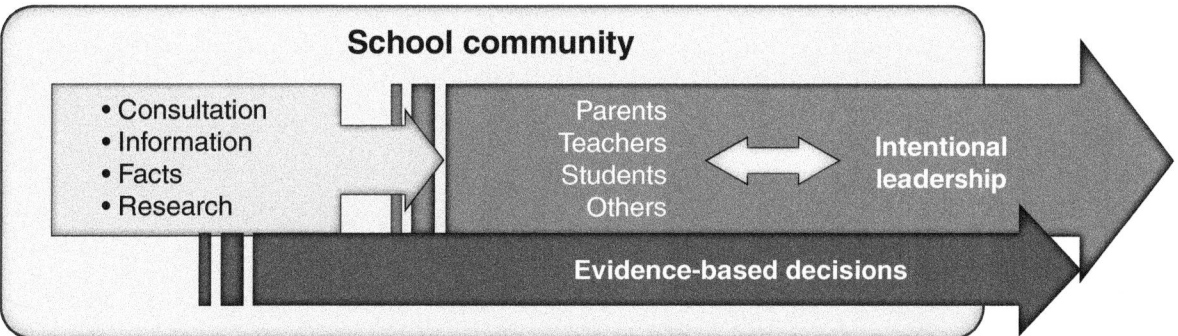

Figure 3.1 Process for intentional leadership in an education community.

- They meet regularly with staff and attend the majority of staff professional development sessions, ensuring that they are aware of and understand the various stages, challenges and needs of staff.

- They provide information to other staff and support the implementation process so that the teaching team is not placed under any undue scrutiny or criticism from other staff during the initial implementation stages.

- They do not hedge their bets—that is, they do not sit on the fence, claiming that a school can operate successfully with more than one philosophy.

Effective and ongoing evaluation and assessment of the approach in relation to teaching and learning should be built into the process. This is usually through an action research model that uses not only data from testing, but focus group discussions with students, parents and teachers along with anecdotal observations, longitudinal collection of additional skills such as social skills, motivation and engagement.

We recommend leaders avoid…

- a culture that endorses the mindset that each teacher can just teach the way they prefer

- allowing individual teachers to make decisions about the future direction of a school's philosophy and pedagogy. This is an open invitation for a teacher who finds change difficult to resist and often obstruct an entire school or team from effectively being able to implement the approach

- trying to reach a consensus among an entire school community about the direction for the teaching and learning. Leadership actually needs (after due and respectful dialogue and discussion with others) to make a decision and set the direction

- trying to have bits and pieces of lots of different pedagogies. This is a recipe for disaster. It gives confusing and mixed messages to parents, teachers and students and does not provide a seamless or consistent set of teaching and learning strategies across a school community.

Fact finding: Clarity rather than assumptions

Many hundreds of staff attend professional development programs to find out about the WLA. This is part of fact finding, staff discussion and information gathering. It is interesting to note here that at the conclusion of a session, staff often make the comment, 'I wish my principal had been here, they don't understand about this at all.' We always recommend that the principal or someone from leadership attends an information session in the early 'fact-finding' period. Leadership attendance ensures that all staff, particularly those with decision-making abilities, are aware of and have received the same information. In addition, we often meet with the leadership team at the school, to ensure they know about the approach and what we recommend as a series of strategies for effective implementation.

Fact finding is an important part of making sure that any approach a school is thinking of putting into practice is well researched, based on sound theory, practical to implement and consistent with state, territory or national framework requirements. With any approach, there are people who think they may know or have heard about it, or claim to have tried it, without ever reading a book, reviewing the research or being provided with support, mentoring and professional development. This can be a dangerous situation; misunderstandings and a lack of knowledge about the approach can lead to inappropriate and poorly constructed practices, which in turn are ineffective in the teaching and learning process. Not only is this undesirable for the children, it can also increase the likelihood of giving the approach a negative reputation, despite the fact that the staff weren't actually using the approach as it was intended.

While we always encourage teachers to add their own particular skills and tools to the WLA, we do not endorse teachers changing and altering the approach to the point where the key elements that have been researched for over a decade cease to exist. This undermines the integrity and rigour of the approach. An educational philosophy and pedagogy is a science, and in the case of the WLA it has taken many years to develop, trial, research and review the approach to ensure that teaching and learning is enhanced rather than compromised. The WLA is far more complex than many teachers assume and ensuring that leadership and staff are aware of the how, what and why of it all, is a critical part of the early days before implementation.

Our key point here is to ensure that you find out the facts and work toward shared understandings across the school or team, which will help to avoid myths, misinterpretations and/or ignorance.

Creating an implementation plan

Once the fact-finding has been completed and the leadership and staff have made a commitment to implement the approach, we recommend a number of key strategies during the process. It is important to recognise that implementing an actual pedagogy as opposed to a discrete program requires forward planning, time and support.

In this process, Stages 1 and 2 are the most important; these recommended processes are considered to be the ideal preparation and support for successful implementation of the WLA. Stages 3 and 4 are additional options for schools/staff wishing to proceed further.

Stage 1

- All team members who will be implementing the approach: (i) attend an information symposium, (ii) visit a school with accredited teachers implementing the approach and/or (iii) attend a two-day study tour (descriptions of these professional development sessions are provided in Table 3.1).

- Leadership attends a symposium or an introductory overview session as a leadership team.

- At least 6 months lead-in time of preparation allowed before actual implementation.

- A whole-school overview of the WLA is conducted at a staff meeting after school or during a professional development session.

- A parent information session conducted by WLA staff is provided for further input and information sharing with the wider community.

Stage 2

- Mentoring—with a WLA accredited mentor who has implemented the approach in their own classroom as a teacher—commences.

  - Mentoring provides assistance and information on planning, linking to literacy and numeracy, ensuring curriculum framework outcomes are met, learning environment set-up, resourcing, modelling ERP sessions and communication board and room set-up.

  - Mentoring consists of a mix of discussions as well as model teaching in the classroom, observations and debriefs.

  - Two mentor sessions are recommended for the teaching team in the term before implementation.

- Three mentor sessions per term are recommended for the first year and two or three sessions in the second year. (For rural, remote and regional schools these are usually conducted in either whole day, half-day or 3-hour sessions combined with distance education support.)

- Regular updates with leadership team.

- A visit to other schools for observation.

- Sustaining the approach if there are changes in the teaching team or leadership.

- Attend a further study tour once 12 months into implementation.

Stage 3

- Moving the approach into other areas of the school.

- Accrediting staff who are successfully implementing the WLA.

Stage 4

- Being identified as a school to host visitors to model the WLA.

Table 3.1 Professional development opportunities and the WLA

Type of Professional Development	Description of Professional Development
School visits	Schools implementing the WLA throughout Australia, which provide opportunities for teachers to observe the learning environment and talk with teaching and leadership staff. The teachers at these schools are usually accredited in the WLA and visitors are able to talk with them and gain further insights into the approach. Most schools host visitors on days of symposiums.
Study tours (1 or 2 days)	These offer a practical and theoretical immersion in the approach, including professional development sessions alongside visits to at least three schools in either metropolitan Melbourne or rural areas with a range of different socioeconomic and cultural demographics.
Symposiums	Symposiums of either half or full days conducted in all states and territories as either introductory or extension information and professional development sessions.
Whole/half day professional development	Sessions designed to meet the specific needs of the school or network. Sessions are developed from a mix of theoretical, practical and reflective practice and individuated scaffolding.
Whole school overview	Presented to the leadership and teaching team, including coaches and special educators.
Mentoring	With a WLA accredited mentor who has implemented the approach in their own classroom as a teacher. This is a combination of mentoring during and outside class time. Teachers are provided with instruction, model teaching, demonstrations, reflective practice and a scaffolding review. Remote, regional and rural teachers are offered the opportunity for mentoring using a distance education model.
Tele/Skype/video conference mentoring	Useful for any school but particularly for rural, regional and remote schools which are implementing the WLA but are not able to access regular mentoring and professional development due to distance.
Weekend conferences (1 or 2 days)	Generally conducted by organisations or networks of schools—usually a combination of keynote lectures and breakout sessions of practical application including videos of implementation in the classroom.
Group school mentoring	Offered as an additional service to support schools. Group school mentoring provides professional development in one location for teachers from different schools. It is not a replacement for individual school mentoring but does provide some further options for schools seeking to ensure effective and sustained implementation of the WLA. These group sessions are intended to be supplementary and complementary to individual school mentoring.
Parent information sessions	Conducted in the afternoon or evening to help parents understand what effective teaching and learning in the 21st century looks like and how the WLA operates in the classroom.

- Contributing to workshops and conferences.

Timelines

The anticipated timeline for full, successful implementation of the WLA in at least one whole teaching team, or a whole school (depending on the amount of mentoring and professional development as well as the size of the team or school) is usually 12–18 months. Most change theories remind us that effective and sustained change requires time, reflection, evaluation and a period of adjustment (Marion 2002; Mazzuno 2001).

Study tours and professional development sessions

The WLA provides a range of different professional development opportunities to support, strengthen and sustain effective teaching and learning not only in the early stages of implementation but into the future (see Table 3.1).

Preparation and lead time

We recommend that schools or teams spend at least one term (preferably two) in lead time before commencement. So many aspects of the approach require discussion, time and preparation. Gathering of resources, understanding the new planning formats, ensuring these link back to state/territory and national frameworks, commencing mentoring, visiting and observing schools and setting up the learning environment are all required to be organised before the WLA can be successfully implemented.

Mentoring

Through any change process and the acquisition of new information and skills, support from experienced staff is important. Mentoring provides ongoing support to teams and schools implementing the WLA.

WLA mentoring is provided by Early Life Foundations in a range of ways depending on the location, needs and timeline of staff:

- at individual schools in meetings and discussion with teams
- in the classroom (model teaching)
- via Skype and video conferencing/teleconferencing
- group school mentoring (where staff from a few schools are mentored together).

Aspects of mentoring sessions include:

- planning
- environment set-up
- resourcing
- practical ideas
- links to literacy and numeracy
- how to conduct various aspects of the WLA including clinics and ERPs
- timetabling a week
- developmental domains
- links and auditing against state/territory and national framework expectations
- assessment
- documentation
- reporting
- model teaching of an ERP session, student-led conference, class meeting, communication board use, clinic groups.

Parent information

Parents are an integral part of the school community. They not only help to shape policy and directions of a school, in many cases, they are key partners in the learning processes of their children. They must be informed about the teaching and learning strategies being implemented within the school. Parents often expect to see learning look exactly like it did when they were in primary school. They can become confused, fearful or apprehensive if they see or hear about things that appear 'different' from what they believe school and learning should be. We find a series of strategies helps significantly to empower and inform parents and to help them feel at ease with some of the changes they may witness.

- A parent information session conducted by our organisation that helps to set the scene for parents about what teaching and learning needs to look like and provide for young learners moving into their futures. An emphasis is placed on the facts that as educators we still instruct, formally teach literacy and numeracy, set limits and expectations, work within state/territory and national frameworks and in addition provide greater opportunities for children to develop skills that are imperative for success in learning and life (for example, resilience, self-esteem, problem-solving, risk-taking, initiating, decision-making, independence, creative and lateral thinking).

- A parent information section of the communication board which displays plans for each fortnight's learning and photographs of examples of students at work in a variety of different classes.

- A class information session for parents about how the day and week works and how it includes all the key learning expectations.

- Invitations for parents to participate in clinic groups and to take part in ERP sessions.

- A hands-on session where parents are invited to attend and participate in an ERP and clinic group to experience what their children are exposed to and involved with on a daily basis.

- Explanations and descriptions of the approach in detail by leadership and those responsible for school tours and parent interviews.

- Ultranet or website updates and information.

Research and evaluation

Sustained and successful implementation of a new approach requires time and reflection, and will involve successes and challenges throughout the process. The journey will involve moments when people want to give up, and other 'ah ha' moments of realisation and excitement. Part of professional growth and learning for individual teachers, teams and schools as well as the broader education community requires professionals to document the process. This serves a number of significant and helpful purposes:

- evidence of the processes and changes made within a team or school

- identification of the specific challenges which can be used to inform others

- reassurance that progress is being made and tracked

- ideas and suggestions for others

- reminders of what key areas need to be addressed at particular times.

We often suggest additional diagnostic tools can be used in a variety of areas including, social, behavioural, self-esteem and engagement:

- as part of an individual's own professional portfolio

- for use with applications for grants and funds

- as part of professional presentations to other colleagues, conferences.

One of the by-products of working through the implementation process to introduce the WLA is the increased opportunity it provides for staff to reflect on their practices, to revisit and access research and update themselves on teaching and learning strategies and studies. It provides opportunities for staff collectively to discuss, develop stronger shared understandings and to ensure a deeper level of philosophy and pedagogy across an entire school community.

Mapping the journey: A protocol

Change in a school's philosophy and pedagogical approach towards teaching and learning involves a significant and substantial commitment from the school leadership and teaching staff. The change process should be a well-planned and mapped journey. Gathering empirical evidence of any journey is an important part of the planning–evaluating–planning cycle. This evidence should be qualitative and quantitative in nature and should include not just children's outcomes in terms of numeracy and literacy, but build a complete picture of how the change in teaching and learning has influenced the whole child, the teaching group, the leadership and the community.

This protocol is a guideline for how schools can begin to map their journey and collect meaningful and purposeful data. The starting point is most important, as it can be used as the baseline for future projections and reflections; a well characterised beginning allows for good communication of the true essence of the journey's progression.

Collecting data

Preliminary data capture should include:

- context of school
- rationale for wanting to introduce play/active investigation
- current classroom structures and timetable of each day
- current classroom set up (before-and-after photographs are useful)
- reading results as collected by school
- numeracy results as collected by school
- other testing that may be already used by the school or is required by the government.

Additional data that we recommend:

- focus group discussions with parents
- focus group discussions with staff
- focus group discussions with leadership
- diagnostic tools to measure oral language, social skills, engagement, etc. (see recommendations below)
- anecdotal information and feedback from parents and school community including local kindergarten teachers.

Documenting the process of change

This part of the process should include records such as:

- minutes of meetings held with leadership, staff and parents
- number, date and content of professional development sessions
- mentoring experiences
- journal accounts (either electronic, paper or both) which capture the essence of meetings, discussions, changes in planning, timetables, classroom set up, etc. It is important to have both:
  - a main journal for the school or team
  - journals of notes of mentoring sessions, thoughts, changes, challenges and achievements for each individual teacher.

Additional ideas:

- take lots of photos and videos of children (ensuring first that you have parental permission)
- video some of your team discussions, meetings and mentoring sessions
- video tuning in and reflection time for discussion and professional development among the teaching team.

Diagnostic tool recommendations (see References for full details):

- *ASK-KIDS inventory for children* by Dr Laurel Bornholt
- *The Hundred Pictures Naming Test* by John Fisher and Jennifer Glenister
- *Social Skills Improvement System* by Frank Gresham and Stephen Elliott

Summary

Effective and sustained implementation requires:

- leadership support, direction and knowledge

- ongoing support from professionals who are expert in the area

- time for preparation, research and fact-finding

- resourcing

- evaluation

- information sharing with whole school community, including parents.

Chapter 4
Education research projects

'We inevitably doom our children to failure and frustration when we try to set their goals for them.'

Jess Lair

Introduction

Education research projects (ERPs) involve project work jointly chosen by the teacher and student in student-led conferencing and teacher-led group discussions. The ERPs are based on very broad focus goals that may come from the state/territory or national framework discipline areas (e.g., Australian history) and then link directly to specific learning intentions.

Students are required to complete a project proposal which sets out suggested timelines and particular interests within the broad focus; specific goals they wish to work toward; whether they wish to work independently or with another student and how they will present their project. In this approach, students do *not* work on the same topic, for the same length of time with similar outcomes expected. ERPs always include a literacy and numeracy element. Teachers present input sessions to the whole group and individual students to provide guidance and parameters around the focus. It is expected and necessary for teachers to formally model and work through the proposal forms and process with students. This is viewed as a major part of the ERP. The proposal form is an in-depth process that requires teacher input. The proposal form is not intended for students to complete independently, particularly in the first few terms.

Students are given a period of time each week to work on their ERPs. This is usually three or four sessions, including modelling and input from teachers, immersion of information, modelling of skills that may be required and clinic groups.

Specific students are focus students each day who report back and share with their peers their experiences, learning and where they are up to with their ERP. It may be content they share, it may be their challenges, and it may be what they are learning about themselves. It will also include the skills and techniques they are using in research, presentation and data collection/analysis. Focus students feed back to the group each session, thus providing peer scaffolding and tutoring on an increased range of topic areas and information. These sessions may also include peer and self assessment, goal setting and presentation skills.

Essentially, ERPs replace what are often referred to as the traditional integrated studies topics. The benefits of ERPs that have been reported by teachers and students include:

- Flexibility with the length of time of each ERP. There is no need for the project to stretch for a whole ten-week term. Most students would work on two or three projects each term. Realistic timelines set students up to be more likely to succeed.

- Empowerment of the student to choose something that is more genuinely and authentically of interest to them, ensuring increased motivation and higher levels of engagement and being on task.

- Increased amount of actual skills, content and knowledge being shared between students.

- Broader range of issues, concepts and ideas that expand the student's experiences. A much greater level of specific information and skills is covered. For example, 25 projects on 'the gold rush' are avoided!

- An emphasis is placed on the skills of research and presentation. Learning about subjects such as history is not blocked into chunks, thus avoiding comments from students such as 'We did the gold rush this term'.

- The integration of literacy and numeracy skills within the ERP is a key part of the approach. This extends the amount of literacy and numeracy taught as it is included not only in an ERP but also in the daily instruction.

- Empowering students to take responsibilities for discussion, negotiation, risk taking, reflection and self assessment (with the guidance of the teacher). It helps students to reflect and gives students practice with life skills necessary for future work and study.

- Proposal forms, contracts, student-led conferencing and student focus times provide a deep, structured learning approach.

Teachers and schools still have a plan of which subject areas and major goals are to be met each term and these are identified from state or territory frameworks. However, the mentality of the past, 'We are doing the gold rush next term' shifts to 'Our goal is to consider some aspects of early Australian white history in relation to …' Within that perspective, students may choose a range of focus areas or goals that are identified by the teacher. These may also be discussed with other experts in the school, by the students and sometimes parents.

> *The philosophy of the WLA reconceptualises traditional thinking in education from viewing the student as an 'empty vessel' that needs filling with every fact and figure about a topic, to a more broad-based emphasis of 'How do I find out, what do I need to know, what is important, what skills do I need, what information is relevant for me to know and to share with others?'*
> *This is achieved while specific information or requirements from frameworks are still being covered.*

In this chapter we provide a detailed unpacking of education research projects, including understanding the purpose of the ERP, detailed descriptions of each element of the ERP, how to introduce ERPs to students and how to develop proposals, contracts and other aspects of the ERP.

ERPs at a glance

- At least 3–4 ERP sessions of at least 1.5 hours are provided each week.

- Proposals, contracts and timelines are developed by the student with the teacher and whole and small groups for first 3–6 sessions.

- The ERP time commences with a 15–20 minute whole group session. The teacher scaffolds other information, skills and/or requirements for the session as well as which clinic groups will be conducted during that time or later in the day.

- In the first few weeks of each term, a longer tuning in time is used for immersion, information, modelling and discussion.

- Students work on the ERPs and focus students conduct student-led conferences with their teacher of about 5–10 minutes (usually 2 or 3 students each session).

- Excursions, incursions and information sharing are part of the ERP process.

Teacher role during ERP time

- modelling, scaffolding and directing

- input of information, facts, knowledge

- signing off proposals and contracts

- running at least one clinic group

- working specifically with focus students for their student-led conference re: their ERP and their progress

- identifying specific goals.

Student role during ERP time

- to ensure timelines are on track

- work on ERP

- conduct conference with teacher if focus student

- self assessment/peer assessment

- feedback to whole group at reflection time (at the end of the day).

Unpacking ERPs

Purpose

ERPs are designed for students to have opportunities to explore some of their own interests but to ensure that they also link to framework outcomes in specific subject areas such as history, health, or economics. ERPs are designed to provide authentic engagement, practice in making choices, taking responsibility, investigating and researching, and to provide practice in independent work as well as group work, self and peer assessment. ERPs also embed an integrated element of literacy and numeracy within the project.

The difference between ERPs and traditional integrated studies topics

The WLA ERPs offer some significant differences from traditional integrated studies units and other approaches that start with specific topics predetermined by scope and sequence charts which span across grades for many years.

ERPs do not start with a predetermined topic. Topics such as 'living things', 'rock pools' or 'mini beasts' are not required within an ERP. This does not mean students may not be exploring some of these, but if they do, it will be from very different perspectives, starting points and expectations. Traditional predetermined topics (particularly very narrow ones such as rock pools) assume that all students will be interested in and should learn a particular amount of *content* related to rock pools. This also assumes that the content and understanding about something like rock pools is important for students to know about.

Teaching and learning in the 21st century is not about learning prescriptive and narrow content on a predetermined topic. Rather, it is *concepts* that children need to be introduced and exposed to; to understand and learn about. Teaching and learning concepts emphasises not only understanding and some knowledge, but more importantly, helps students engage and produce skills in research, exploration and translating information into new and different circumstances. Teaching transferable skills is an essential element in any effective pedagogy so that students can see the links between skills and knowledge that may be useful in other areas of life and learning. It is unnecessary for students in the 21st century to be filled with information about rock pools. It is however, useful to be introduced to and find some degree of relevant information and understanding about systems, environment, history, ecology and health.

In other words, having 23 students all produce similar content-based projects on the same questions limits learning to predetermined answers and content. The starting point for a team or teacher in determining an ERP focus is not with a topic, but a set of key objectives or intentions based on a specific subject focus.

The language used in the WLA in literacy, numeracy and ERPs never includes anything described as 'doing'. We don't 'do', literacy, numeracy or government; the language would never include, 'We are doing government this term'. The language that is used in the WLA incorporates learning, such as:

Key learning intentions as identified from framework:

For children to understand about governing, how communities and people make decisions, the different types of governments that exist and relevant terms such as 'democracy'.

Starting with a subject focus rather than a topic immediately broadens the notion of what will be researched and investigated and provides a wider range of choice for students when they come to their actual project.

If a teaching team are not clear what the learning objectives actually are and how they link to framework learning intentions, then a vital ingredient is missing. If teachers are not clear, then students won't be either! Starting with a subject focus and associated intentions makes very clear what and why the learning intentions are, how they relate to the framework expectations and also reminds teachers, parents and students that learning about and understanding particular concepts is far more complex, interesting and diverse than studying a predetermined topic such as minibeasts.

Working from a subject focus also ensures that students and teachers concentrate on the skills and learning required to meet outcomes and explore issues rather than to simply replicate lots of information about a topic.

Key points

Education research projects:

- *still reflect and relate to specific subjects and outcomes as required in frameworks*
- *emphasise a broader range of skills and concepts than working from predetermined topics*
- *provide a more authentic and wider choice for students in their projects*
- *give greater clarity about learning objectives*
- *emphasise the process of research, links to own prior knowledge and the processes of investigating, discussion and self responsibility for students*
- *link in specific elements of literacy and numeracy skills and expectations*
- *provide a broad range of ways in which students can demonstrate their project.*

ERP sessions: How often and when?

In the early years of school, at least four morning investigation sessions are recommended each week. The increased maturity and cognitive development in students in the middle and upper years of primary school provides greater flexibility as to when ERP sessions are conducted. Older children are more able to adapt and do not need to have an ERP time at the same time in the morning every day. Generally three or four ERP sessions (a minimum of three) are held across each week at any time that fits within timetabling.

Understanding the ERP process

Before the term commences the teaching team:

1. decides on the subject focus for the term (this may have been determined across the school)

2. identifies the key learning intentions, concepts and issues for students' goals from the relevant framework.

Commencement of term

General preliminary discussion

The teacher discusses current interests of the children before introducing the key subject focus and learning intentions. This is to ensure that teachers are receiving input from students about their real and current interests. These interests may initially have nothing to do with the subject focus and this is exactly as it should be; it helps to avoid predetermining an agenda and allows students to fully explore their own current interests.

Presenting the subject focus and learning intentions for the term

Once the general discussion and sharing of ideas and interests has occurred, the teacher then moves into presenting a brief overview of the subject focus and key learning intentions for the students.

It may sound like this:

> *'It's been good to hear what your interests are; I know some of you are still thinking about your interests and how your interests may inform some of our discussions over the next few weeks and what your project may involve. Our subject focus this term is Australian history and the key issues, ideas and learning intentions we have identified that need to be included this term are...'*

Linking interests with subject focus and learning intentions

This is a critical aspect of the approach. Instead of fitting the children around a topic, we need to try to fit the learning intentions and subject focus around the children's interests. This is authentic, differentiated and personalised learning which retains specific learning intentions. For example, Kathy is interested in sailing. The question to ask is: 'Can Kathy's interest in sailing link somehow to the learning intentions and early Australian history?' The answer is sometimes 'Yes'.

Sometimes we may not find a link that is substantial enough to have possibilities to link to the learning intention.

For some children, they may not even be able to identity an interest in the first place. This is not a problem, as the teacher will still guide, scaffold, introduce and shape ideas for students who need help. Once a suitable interest has been established, the question becomes, 'How can Kathy's interest in sailing and her desire to complete a project on boats demonstrate learning related to the intentions and subject focus of the term?'

Immersion and discussion phase

This is a very important part of the term. Whole-class and clinic groups as well as individual discussions will take place during ERP sessions where the teacher will involve children in lots of information, exposure, resources, excursions and incursions related to the key concepts and learning

Table 4.1   A proposal form with notes in each section to help guide the teacher in supporting students in the planning process

Education Research Project (ERP) Student Proposal		the Walker Learning Approach DEVELOPMENTALLY APPROPRIATE PRACTICE
Student name:	**Term:**	**Date:**
Project Scope		
Major subject focus	The team, school or year level may have a particular subject area from the state or national framework each term as a focus (e.g., Australian history). Some schools use a mix of different subjects within each term; other schools prefer to have one discrete subject focus each term.	
Key interest area Why are you interested?	The student writes about or describes their own particular interest. This is done before the subject focus and intentions are shared with students. The student must describe the personal side of their choice.	
How does your interest link to the subject focus and learning intentions?	The student must provide justification here on how their interest and project will fulfil some of the expected intention criteria as identified by the teacher at the commencement of the term.	
What are you hoping to find out?	The student must identify some key points of what they are particularly hoping to establish or find out more about, or check out what they think they already know. They may pose a question or hypothesis or they may wish to explore and test the history or knowledge.	
Suggested timeline	The student is allowed to choose the length of the project (with teacher input). It is usually about 4–6 weeks but may differ dependent on student needs/strengths.	
Will you be working in a team or on your own? What is your reason for choosing to work alone or in a team?	To be able to work independently and interdependently are both valued as important aspects of a successful learner. Sometimes the project may be a sole project. Other times the student may negotiate to work with someone else or a small team. Each member of the team must complete their own individual proposal and contract. The student must provide a rationale for their choice.	
In which ways will you present your project?	The student must produce some form of end product. It may be a film, movie, animation, PowerPoint presentation, poster, community service project, play, song, music, etc. It may involve the completion of more than one piece of work; this can also be negotiated. In most cases, the proposal, the contract and at least one written page is required in addition to the end product.	
Ways in which the project may be useful to others (will it have a link to the community?)	The project may (but not necessarily) sometimes involve support from or links to the community. It will at the very least have some relevance to the class but it may extend to the wider school community, local community or beyond.	

Engagement Matters

Table 4.1 continued

	Additional Learning
What aspects of literacy will be included in your project?	The project must include at least one aspect of literacy. It may be a specific genre of writing. It may include a text or references. It may involve a handwritten piece or a report. This may be personalised for each student or reflect a general aspect of literacy being learned during that term.
What aspects of numeracy will be included in your project?	The project must also include at least one element of numeracy. This may be some data collection, graphing, or other mathematical aspect which can be integrated into the project. This may be personalised for each student or reflect a general aspect of numeracy being learned during that term.
Any other subject areas or skills that will be included in your project?	There will be additional skills, information and learning that occur during the course of the project. What other skills does the student anticipate may be acquired (e.g., writing a script)?
List your personal goals for this project	In addition to the project itself and the literacy and numeracy goals, an important aspect of the ERP is the expectation that the student will also acquire some personal skills or set some goals. It may be to adhere to timelines, it may include being able to negotiate or work more collaboratively with others. It may be to stay focused and work independently.
What skills do you already have that will help you with this project?	This provides the student with the opportunity to work from their strengths and to be reflective about their strengths and challenges.
Are there any challenges or difficulties you can think of that are related to this project?	There may be some aspects of the process or the project (recognised from past learning experiences) that the student identifies in advance as possible challenges. These may help to formulate the student's personal goals. It also provides the opportunity for the student and teacher to plan clinic groups that develop and extend these skills.

intentions of the subject focus. If there are certain facts and figures required within the learning intentions, these are shared with students instead of wasting their time in 'finding out' when we actually already have the answers.

In parallel with this phase, discussions continue with students to help them firm up what their ERP will be based on, and how it relates either to their own interest or to an interest that has been generated through the immersion phase. The immersion phase also provides formal instruction and skills in research, finding out and accessing resources.

The proposal form

Filling out the proposal form also commences during the immersion phase. Students complete these in whole groups and clinic groups or individually during student conferencing time with the teacher. It is not expected that the students are competent enough to complete the proposal form on their own; it is part of the learning that students work through the proposal form with support.

The proposal process is in itself a very major part of instruction, planning, identifying ideas and linking back to learning outcomes, not only in the subject focus but in literacy and numeracy. Table 4.1 is an example of a proposal form with notes in each section to help guide the teacher in supporting students in this process. The format and content of the proposal form has been trialled for a number of years with different groups and we do not recommend that teachers modify the form. It is quite a complex form and therefore teachers must be explicit and instructive in how to complete it. Filling in the proposal form is an integral aspect of teaching and learning—it should not be viewed as an interruption or a quick one-hour fill-in-the-boxes exercise.

Students do not have to have completed every single aspect of the proposal form before they commence researching, designing or starting their actual project. The proposal form is a work in progress to some degree; it can be updated, changed or modified. But it is intended to clarify, early in the term, the key ideas and interest of the project, how it links to the learning intentions and a suggested timeline.

The contract

This is signed off during the term in recognition that the student has completed and discussed all aspects of the proposal process. The student does not have to wait until the contract has been signed to commence their project but it is anticipated that the contract may be signed off during one of the student-led conferences; this provides a sense of achievement, agreement and accountability. The contract terms can be negotiated and changed if required in agreement with and authorisation by the teacher. A sample contract form can be found in the Appendices and on the CD.

How does a teaching team plan for the ERP each term?

Each school or team may have a particular way of organising how they move through the various subject areas required by state or national frameworks. We recommend that a school or team simply considers the range of key learning intentions and subject requirements for a particular grade or level and organises each term to have a specific subject focus. Some schools may wish to choose two subject areas. It is up to schools and teams how comfortable they feel assessing and auditing learning intentions as required by framework expectations. Traditional planning days will still provide the time and opportunity to pre-plan excursions, resources and ideas.

Schedule of ERP events

Week 1: Session 1

Introduction: Whole group discussion

'What have you been doing over the holidays? What current interests do you have? Do you have any ideas of what types of projects you might like to work on this term?' This discussion deliberately does not start with the subject focus or intentions. It provides some opportunity for authentic interests of the children to be shared. It doesn't mean all interests can be used or will fit within the scope of the subject focus but it allows free discussion and exploration.

Introduction to subject focus and intentions

The teacher informs the children of the subject focus and associated key learning intentions that are being explored during the term. For example: 'This term our focus is taken from the science subject with a focus on the environment. Our key learning intentions include:

- examining aspects of man-made and natural environments and how environments are impacted on by human intervention

- how natural environments impact on other living things

- how man-made environments may impact on climate, health and population.'

Exploring students' interests

The teacher needs to work out how and if students' authentic interests can relate or lend themselves to exploring and meeting some of the intentions within the subject focus. For example: 'Jamie, you said you had visited the "Wet 'n' Wild" theme park in Queensland and you were interested in some sort of ERP about that. Can you or can anyone else think of how Jamie's interest could fit within our major focus and intentions?'

'I could look at the theme park and what difference it has made since it was built and what was there naturally before it was made. Or, I could look at the use of water and if they recycle it and what that means to the environment.'

Students are encouraged to think and discuss, and to work in small groups to brainstorm interests and any links they can initially think of between the intentions and their real interests. The teacher models, suggests, directs and scaffolds during this process.

Following weeks: Sessions 2, 3 and onwards

Continuation of session 1

Identifying interests with teacher direction that may link to intentions and subject focus.

Immersion phase of information and concepts commences

In this part of the sessions, teachers provide input about the subject and related ideas and concepts. Incursions, excursions, videos, texts, websites, information and other visiting experts are provided, particularly over the first two or three weeks to introduce students to certain aspects that relate broadly to the intentions and information. For example, a visitor may speak to the whole class about water conservation, the class may visit a particular site or organisation, and videos may be shown. A parent who has a particular level of expertise in either the subject focus or in skills that may be useful for completion of projects may be invited to contribute. Students are not required to identify key understandings or questions as a whole group. This is unnecessary as the proposal phase personalises these within the broader intentions expected.

The immersion phase is most concentrated in the first two to three weeks. This assists students who may be having difficulty in identifying a particular project as well as providing lots of the information, facts and figures that are required to be covered. The WLA does not endorse wasting students' time by having them research facts and figures that are readily available and accessible. If there are dates or events that need to be included, just tell them during the immersion phase. The students will have plenty of time to be researching in more authentic ways based on their own interests once they start their projects.

Each ERP session may involve or include some further immersion, information sharing from the teacher or others. However, as the first few weeks evolve, students are starting to work on their own projects, complete proposal forms, research, discuss with the teacher individually as well as to be part of clinic groups that will focus on either information or skills related to the subject focus or the individual ERPs.

Following sessions

ERP session format summary

- *Tuning in (teacher input): may include formal information, ideas, modelling of various parts of the proposal form, facts, figures, research skills, ideas for presentations, making links to literacy and numeracy*
- *independent and/or group work*
- *clinic groups*
- *student-led conferencing during ERP with teacher*

Each session commences with further input and information sharing from the teacher. It also provides time for students to complete their proposal forms and work on their projects.

Tuning in at the beginning of the day involves three or four focus students sharing with the whole class what they are working on, their goals, timelines and information they are gathering. The aims here include content and information sharing across the greater class, speaking, listening and reflecting in front of the group. Having focus students report back to the class each day also builds in some accountability—while they have choice about their actual project, they are still required to report, reflect, produce and learn specific aspects related to learning intentions and the subject focus.

Clinic groups may be held during ERP time either by the teacher or other staff, parents or community members that relate to either the actual project or subject focus information, or skills that may be useful for the project.

Student-led conferencing also occurs: this is where the teacher and individual students will meet during ERP time to focus on a range of issues such as proposal forms, timelines, content, skills and the project itself.

Each day finishes with reflection time, when students come back to consider what has occurred during the day. Focus students in particular are expected to reflect on their learning during the

ERP session and in the progress of their project. This is where challenges, personal reflections, gains, learning and other associated issues can be raised. It is a time where other students listening are encouraged to participate, to ask questions and seek further ideas.

What is the role of the teacher?

The teacher has a range of roles related to the ERP process. These include:

- introducing the subject focus and identifying learning objectives

- providing opportunities for open discussion and exploration of students' own interests

- making links to learning intentions based on students' interests

- teaching skills related to timelines, researching, ways of producing projects

- mapping and tracking focus students

- modelling and providing input to key elements of proposal forms

- providing information and relevant incursions, excursions

- organising/running clinic groups

- ensuring student-led conferencing occurs with all students each week or fortnight.

Focus students

We recommend each student is a focus once a fortnight. This ensures that no student falls between the gaps. It helps students to take responsibility for their learning, to keep to their timelines, and to gain some individual one-on-one time with the teacher.

Focus students understand that they have to reflect in front of the group about their project, the proposal forms, their interests and the information they are gaining.

We strongly suggest a focus student roster system, displayed on the communication board so students (and their parents) are aware of when it will be their turn to present.

Timelines of projects

The WLA aims to ensure that each individual student is respected and provided with as many opportunities as possible to succeed in their learning. The WLA philosophy accepts that some students will require less or more time with their actual project than others. Therefore, part of the proposal form allows for, and encourages the teacher and the student to consider, what length of time their project may last. Generally speaking a student will have two projects each term. However, some may have only one, and some students may have three.

The key learning intentions and subject focus are the major emphasis in the first project of each student. If there is more than one project per term, it is up to the discretion of the teacher as to whether the second project needs to meet the learning intentions and subject focus or whether there may be a wider range of choice for the student. In these subsequent projects, the proposal form must still be completed albeit at a more simplistic level.

The issue is not how long a student worked on a project per se; but rather, how relevant, purposeful, productive and engaged the student was and how the learning actually occurred.

Student-led conferencing

During the ERP session, focus students (and/or others as designated by the teacher or requested by the student) are involved in student-led conferencing. During these conferences, the student is required to talk with and discuss various elements of the project with their teacher. It is deliberately called a student-led conference to encourage the student to take some leadership and set some of the direction, questions and issues of the discussion. The teacher also naturally raises issues, ideas and may set new directions, expectations and any other relevant considerations.

Immersion

As discussed above, this is the key information-sharing phase where teachers and teams provide information, facts, figures, ideas and opportunities to find out that relate to the subject focus and learning intentions. It is the period of time (mostly at the beginning of a term, but also throughout the term) where students are provided with information and concepts that they may be less familiar with. It reflects the idea that children don't know what they don't know. It gives teachers permission to expose students to and inform them of other ideas and related concepts that are deemed relevant and useful. It does not however, focus on a narrow topic or set of facts.

Incursions and excursions

It is anticipated that teachers will use a range of people, organisations, experiences, facts, figures, information and content as appropriate during the process.

Using the proposals

The proposal forms are in-depth, considered and evolving; it is not expected or desirable that students are simply handed the proposal form and told to go away and complete it.

The proposal forms are modelled, worked through as a whole group, in clinic groups and individually. Some teachers use an electronic whiteboard to do this. Some teachers link the filling out of the form back into literacy and numeracy sessions. The process involves joint discussion, idea sharing, identification of timelines and scaffolding by the teacher as to what types of links may be included.

Student ERP journal

This is where the proposal contract and any work, information, thoughts and ideas are collected as part of the student's learning.

The expo

The expo is held once a term. It is organised and conducted by the students (albeit with some support and modelling from the teacher/team). Aims of the expo are to provide students with the opportunity to:

- show leadership in organising and conducting a community event
- plan, invite, schedule and set up a community event (including catering and invitations where possible)
- share their learning, thinking, interests, proposals and processes of learning
- speak publicly and demonstrate presentation skills.

For the community, the aims are to:

- learn and share in how students are learning
- participate in a community school-based event
- understand more fully the richness and diversity in teaching and learning
- learn about and experience key interests and concepts of students.

The expo is most commonly held toward the last few weeks of each term to provide as much time as possible for students to have fully engaged in their project. It is not necessary that a finished project be ready for the expo. In fact, the process, information and skills acquired along the way are an important part of the expo.

Key steps for conducting the expo

- Planning of the expo commences almost at the beginning of each term.
- Students discuss and plan; an expo committee of students and teacher may be formed. While all students will participate in the expo, a small sub-group may take on the extra responsibility of organising the event. This group will change each term to ensure all students have the opportunity to be involved in the organisation.
- A date, time and venue are decided on.
- A list of who will be invited is made (for example, local councillors, particular organisations in the community, parents,

teachers and students from across the school).

- Invitations are designed, made and sent out.

- Catering is decided on. Students may cook, or the school may help with arrangements.

- A program for the expo is made (welcome, announcements, overview of the subject focus).

- The hall or room is set up in individual work stations or booths.

- One or two of the students are designated to open the expo and welcome guests. The principal or teacher also contributes.

- Each student stands beside or behind their area with a small display. This may include: the proposal form, the main project ideas, the learning they have acquired or are still working on, actual examples of the project (a puppet play, a PowerPoint presentation on a laptop, a 3D building or artefact, a video they have made, a poster, a cookbook they may have made).

- Each student is expected to provide a verbal outline of major aspects of their project which they will have prepared beforehand. Key issues to be included:

  - what their initial interest was

  - how it links to subject focus and intentions

  - what their project involves

  - the proposal form and timelines

  - aspects of literacy and numeracy that are included

  - what they have learned, enjoyed and found challenging.

- One or two students close the expo with a short concluding statement and thanks, alongside the teacher or principal.

- Sometimes a guest may be asked to comment on the expo.

Summary

- The teacher still directs, sets learning intentions, scaffolds, introduces concepts, skills and ideas.

- Learning intentions and subject focus are the starting points for each term.

- Students' authentic interests are used as a starting point and links are made where applicable.

- Three or four ERP sessions are conducted at any time during each week.

- Proposal forms are completed with support from the teacher over a period of time.

- Specific information/knowledge related to subject focus and intentions is provided by the teacher.

- Focus students on a roster system share and reflect on their ERP learning to the whole group.

- An expo is held to celebrate the work and learning of the children as well as to provide opportunities for leadership, organisation and shared learning with the wider community.

Subject Focus & Learning Intentions

Subject Focus Planner
Level Three: Term 3 2010

Subject Focus: The Arts

Learning Intentions:

- Students identify techniques and aspects of other people's works that inform their own art
- Students use arts elements, skills, techniques and processes to create and present work that communicates ideas and feelings for different purposes and audiences

...cation Research Project (ERP) Intentions

...s to:

...skills and techniques used by another artist and reflect these in their own

...e of arts skills and techniques to make and present work that conveys a
...o an audience.

Weekly

	Monday	Tuesday
9.00 am	Tuning in	Tuning in
	Literacy Session	Library
10.00 am	Literacy Session Clinic Group	Library
11.00 am		
11:30 pm	Numeracy Session Clinic Group	Sport
1.00 pm		
1.45 pm	ERP	Literacy Clinic Group
2.00 pm	ERP	ERP Clinic Group
3.00 pm	Reflection	Reflection

Statement of Intent

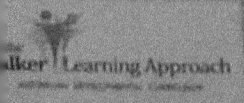

Term:	Subject Focus: Society and Environment
Key Learning Outcomes Identified:	
For the students to:	
• Understand and describe the differences and issues related to manmade and natural environments	
• Identify how some decisions are made and the processes by which they are made which impact upon different environments and communities	

Statement of Intent Grades 3-6

Commencing Fortnight Date: Monday 2nd August   Weeks: 3 & 4

Developmental Domain Focus	Learning Intentions / Outcomes State/National Framework	Immersion or other exposure / concepts, excursion, school, comments, events	Assessment / Reflection Experiences	Learning Experiences	Modifications
...nal	**Numeracy** For the students to: Demonstrate ability to use decimal point ... Use multiplication to...	Swimming carnival Excursion to Museum Mother's day	Portfolio pieces in biography Rubric for self assessment in ERP	Students will: • Revisit costing of their ERP • Write about their ERP using...	This is added to as fortnight progresses

Chapter 5
Planning and documentation

'There is work that is work and there is play that is play; there is play that is work and work that is play. And in only one of these lies happiness.'

Frank Gelett Burgess

Introduction

The success of the WLA is underpinned by intentional, rigorous and detailed planning. This planning ensures that teachers clearly articulate learning objectives related to developmental domains, numeracy, literacy, other subject and associated concepts and state/territory or national framework requirements. It should emphasise emergent and core curriculums, and utilise individual record sheets to craft child-centred individuated teaching and learning.

This chapter provides explanations and examples of the intentional, rigorous and detailed planning that underpins the success of the WLA. It unpacks examples of the range of ways that planning, documenting learning and observations can be used as part of the teaching and learning process.

WLA planning tools

WLA planning always starts with the individual and moves towards the learning objective—this is the reverse to many other planning approaches. In common with all teaching and learning plans, the WLA employs year and term planners or menus. But what makes the WLA unique is the further development of a fortnightly 'statement of intent', individual record sheets and continual qualitative and quantitative assessment tools. In this chapter we will unpack the elements of planning and documentation that are required in order to ensure key learning intentions are tracked for each grade, team and individual student. These include:

- term subject focus and key learning intentions
- term literacy and numeracy intentions or goals
- fortnightly statement of intent (SOI)
- focus student roster
- clinic groups
- individual record (IR) pro forma
- ERP proposal form
- ERP contract
- weekly timetable
- fortnightly key learning intentions in student-friendly language
- portfolios
- daily record sheet/memory jogger.

Term subject focus and key learning intentions

The term subject focus and learning intentions document provides general information about which subject is the focus for the term and lists the key learning intentions that have been identified by the teaching team. This is the starting point of all planning for the term. Starting with a subject focus and associated learning intentions makes it very clear why and what the learning intentions actually are, how they relate to the framework expectations, and also to remind teachers, parents and students of the importance of learning about and understanding *concepts* rather than predetermined *topics*. Once the subject and intentions have been identified, the learning intentions are communicated in student-friendly language (see 'Learning intentions student version' on p. 61). The sequence of events that teachers follow to appropriately identify the term subject focus and key learning intentions is demonstrated in Figure 5.1.

The term subject focus and learning objectives are displayed on the communication board. An example of the document is detailed in Table 5.1 below, and there is a template in the Appendices and on the CD.

Term literacy and numeracy intentions or goals

This is simply a list or table of the key literacy and numeracy learning goals or intentions that the teaching team anticipates will be covered during the term (as identified by the school and from state/territory or national frameworks). These intentions are displayed on the communication board (refer to Chapter 2). These are taken directly from the term numeracy and literacy planner.

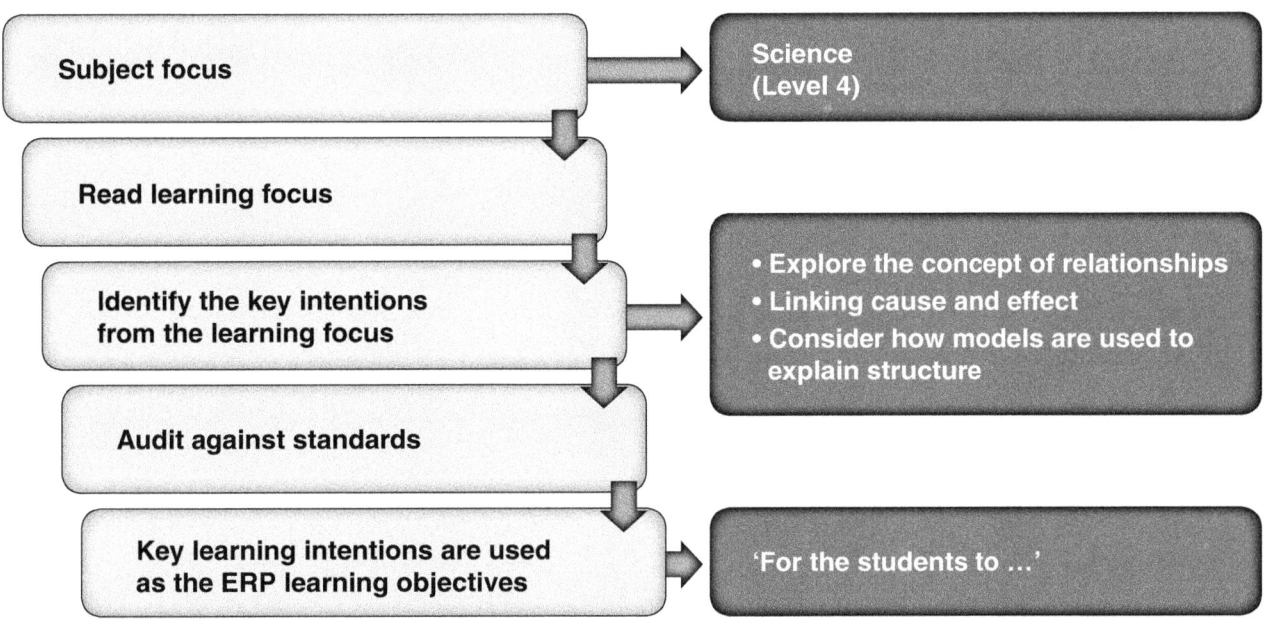

Figure 5.1 Process for constructing ERP term subject learning intentions

Table 5.1 Term subject focus and key learning intentions

Subject Focus and Key Learning Intentions	
Term 1	**Subject Focus: Society and environment**
Subject description or focus areas (taken from framework): This area of study aims to provide students with a greater understanding of how the environment and communities are influenced by both natural environments as well as intervention by society and human influence. It aims to help students understand the implications of and issues related to how environments and communities are influenced and what occurs when these influences impact directly on different environments.	
Key learning intentions identified: For the students to: • understand and describe the differences and issues related to man-made and natural environments • identify how some decisions are made and the processes by which they are made which impact on different environments and communities • provide examples and evidence of their understanding and learning about how the environment and community are influenced by decisions as well as natural events	

Fortnightly statement of intent (SOI)

The statement of intent (SOI) is a key part of planning; it is a dynamic, relevant and responsive planner that can in most instances replace the traditional weekly work plan.

It is called a statement of intent for two main reasons:

1. It provides a formal set of learning intentions in all areas of development and learning (including literacy and numeracy) that are the primary focus for the coming fortnight. It breaks down into specific areas what aspects of learning can be introduced, revised or focused on in the next fortnight. It draws on term goals but is more responsive to additional or different needs of the students that may arise.

2. It reminds a teacher that just because something is written in a plan, doesn't mean it has been 'done', learned or achieved. The term 'intention' rather than 'outcome' is important for effective evaluation and reflection on future planning in the teaching and learning cycle.

The fortnightly SOI has key areas that are completed, modified, added to or deleted in a

Table 5.2 An example of a completed fortnightly statement of intent (SOI)

the Walker Learning Approach — Statement of Intent Grades 3–6	Term:		Subject focus: Society and Environment		
	Key learning intentions identified: For the students to: • understand and describe the differences and issues related to man-made and natural environments • identify how some decisions are made and the processes by which they are made that impact on different environments and communities				
Commencing Date: Monday 4th October, Weeks 1 and 2					
Developmental domain focus	Learning outcomes (state/national framework)	Immersion or other exposure, concepts, excursions, school events	Assessment/ reflection experiences	Learning experiences	Modifications
Emotional For the students to: • express their own feelings and responses in appropriate interactions with others Social For the students to: • contribute ideas to their peers Language For the students to: • use creative and expressive language in their descriptions and discussions Cognitive/Thinking For the students to: • consider perspectives of others alongside their own Physical/Health For the students to: • develop a healthy perspective of image and body	Numeracy For the students to: • demonstrate ability to use decimal point • use multiplication in relation to money Literacy For the students to: • use persuasive text and expression • deepen their understanding of writing a biography Other subjects	• swimming carnival • excursion to Museum • local politics on agenda for class meeting Students' interests • Harry Potter • Mary Poppins • Street party • Fishing • Dancing	• portfolio pieces in biography • rubric for self assessment in ERP	Students will • review costing of their ERP • write about their ERP using a persuasive genre • write their autobiography	*This is added to as the fortnight progresses.*

Engagement **Matters**

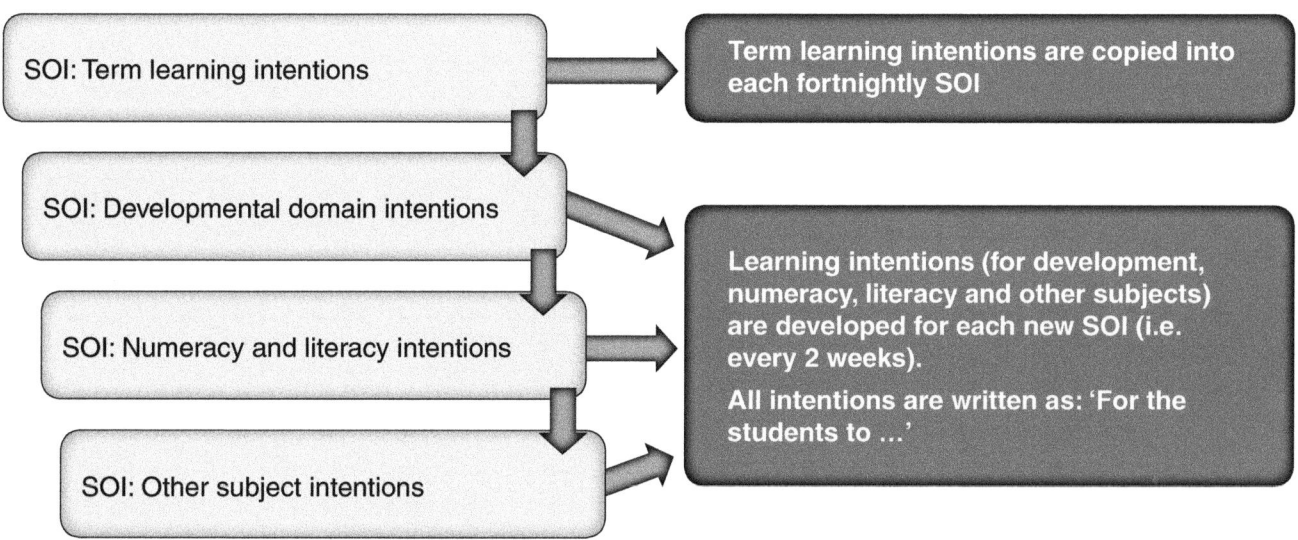

Figure 5.2 Process for teachers constructing fortnightly SOI learning intentions

Note: The term subject focus and term learning intentions remain the same throughout each fortnight for the duration of the term.

fortnightly cycle. Table 5.2 provides an example of a completed SOI. (A blank SOI template is included in the Appendices and on the CD.)

The SOI is printed out (A3 size) each fortnight for display on the communication board (refer to Chapter 2). The aim of the SOI is to communicate to students, parents and the teaching team the key learning intentions, skills and concepts that are being worked on each fortnightly period.

It is highly recommended that the SOI be maintained electronically so that it can be easily modified each fortnight and used as part of an effective cycle of intention, execution and evaluation for future planning.

Significant features of the SOI include:

- identification of aspects of development/life skills
- identification of learning outcomes in literacy, numeracy and any other subject areas
- focus on student/staff/community events
- assessment
- modifications.

Figure 5.2 demonstrates the sequence of tasks that teachers should follow when using the SOI to appropriately identify the term subject focus and key learning intentions (for development, numeracy, literacy and other subjects).

Focus student roster

The focus student roster lists the order in which students will be a focus each fortnight. The aim is that there is some predictability and routine for the students. Obviously there is flexibility with the roster to accommodate the normal day-to-day interruptions and student absences, but it is important that each student is and has a focus each fortnight. The Appendices and CD provide a template for the focus student roster.

Clinic groups

Clinic group pro formas are completed for display on the communication board (refer to Chapters 2 and 4). Students' names are either already on the clinic group lists for each day or week, or there is opportunity for students to register themselves for a specific clinic group. An example of a clinic group timetable is given below, and templates for timetables and sign-up sheets are provided in the Appendices and on the CD.

Table 5.3 Clinic group timetable example

Clinic Group Timetable 		
Day	**Session**	**Type of clinic**
Monday	• Literacy • Numeracy	• Optional clinic: Editing videos • Compulsory clinic: Multiplying decimals
Tuesday	• ERP • Numeracy	• Compulsory clinic: Creative writing • Compulsory Clinics (x 2): Working with percentages
Wednesday	• Numeracy	• Optional clinic: Extending multiplying decimals
Thursday	• Literacy	• Compulsory clinics (x 2): Developing sentence structure
Friday	• ERP	• Optional clinic: Writing poems

Individual record (IR) pro forma

The individual record (IR) pro forma is an important part of the assessing and reporting documentation. The teacher has a file (usually electronic) for each student, and uses it to capture key aspects of learning, development, behaviour, interests and any other information that relates to the student. The teacher completes the form over the course of each term and simply adds in dot-point comments or examples of how and what the student is achieving, doing or needing.

The IR is updated at least 3 times a term for each student and is designed to be a time-efficient document (it should *not* be a time consuming process). The electronic version of the IR means that all information is easily updated; the files just expand and can be added to at any stage. It is used to identify further goals in learning and personalises learning and assessment in an ongoing, dynamic and authentic way.

Key features of the IR include recording:

- development and behaviour including social, emotional, language
- learning examples related to literacy, numeracy and any other subject areas
- goals for learning
- interests
- other relevant information (referrals, recommendations, etc.).

Key uses of the IR include:

- recording individual aspects of learning, behaviour and interests
- developing and updating individual goals for learning
- cutting and pasting text into school reports as 'real' evidence
- individualising learning
- sharing with parents at teacher–student–parent interviews.

The IR should be viewed as an integral part of assessment and evidence of learning. It is highly recommended that teachers have an electronic folder for each student which contains things such as the IR, photos, video clips of learning and interactions (if applicable), samples and evidence of work. An IR template is contained in the Appendices and on the CD.

ERP proposal form

The ERP proposal form is used for teachers and students to work through in planning, negotiating and formulating the final form of the proposal that is signed off as a contract. The ERP proposal form (as explained in detail in Chapter 4) is a major part of the ERP. It is not to be viewed as a quick one-hour project in which students go home and complete the form by themselves. It involves a process of discussion, thinking, negotiating and forms part of learning about a range of key skills and thinking. The Appendices and the CD provide a template for ERP proposal forms (see Table 4.1 for an example of a completed form).

Contract

At some stage in the process during the term, the proposal form will be sufficiently developed so that a contract between the student and the teacher can be signed off—formalising the agreement of what is contained within the proposal. This is a special moment for the student and indicates that the process of thinking, planning and linking to learning intentions and subject focus has been accomplished.

The proposal form may still have bits and pieces to be developed but essentially the teacher and student agree that the key criteria have been identified and the student is now ready for the contract. An template for the contract is in the Appendices and on the CD.

Weekly timetable

The weekly timetable is simply an updated weekly calendar of key events. It may contain some of the clinic group times or specialist classes, etc. that are being held during the week. The weekly timetable is *not* intended to be the planning document; it may remain fairly similar each week or need to be slightly amended. Table 2.1 (in Chapter 2) provides an example of how a weekly timetable may look when implementing the WLA.

Learning intentions (student version)

In addition to the fortnightly SOI, it is recommended that the key learning objectives are listed in student-friendly terms and placed on the communication board (refer to Chapter 2) each fortnight. For example:

> *This fortnight, as identified on our communication board and statement of intent, our major learning intentions include for students to:*
>
> - *demonstrate their ability to understand and apply their knowledge of perimeter*
> - *be introduced to the skills of using decimal points*
> - *use the report writing genre of facts and process/procedure in their literacy*
> - *increase their skills in electronic ways of organising their learning and diaries*
> - *visit the local newspaper for deeper understandings of the role of media in the community.*

A template for this display is also in the Appendices and on the CD.

Portfolios

Portfolios are discussed in detail in Chapter 6. Key features of the portfolios are that they are shared and contributed to by both the student and teacher. There is no secret teacher business! The portfolios record real and authentic examples of learning and are available throughout the year for parents to view. Students are encouraged to contribute to these and identify what they believe is worth capturing.

Daily record sheet/memory jogger

The daily record sheet/memory jogger provides the opportunity for teachers to document things that occur, in order to help them make meaningful links for students; to add or bring in additional resources; to note that they may wish to follow up a discussion; or add a new dimension to a discussion the next day or next ERP session. These prompts may occur at any time during the day; during a clinic group, a whole class session or an ERP session.

Teachers generally do this in their own minds and keep mental notes. The daily record sheet is simply an optional extra that allows for having something down on paper, which some teachers find useful. It is also useful to collate these sheets as a record of spontaneous issues that arise over time. Students can add to the daily record sheet with additional ideas or suggestions.

Summary

WLA planning and documentation is similar to many teaching and learning approaches; however it does have unique characteristics that help teachers reconceptualise their planning away from the topic and content and towards the skills and the individual. These unique characteristics include:

- fortnightly planning through the statement of intent that responds to and reflects on what really happened in each learning cycle

- displaying planning for students, parents and visitors (there is no secret teacher business)

- emphasising individual records and goals that are updated three times each term

- including students in collecting and collating samples of learning

- using student interests and learning intentions as part of the learning and planning cycle

- portfolios that are more student owned and collated and provide flexibility for teachers.

Chapter 6
Assessment and reporting

'To accomplish great things, we must not only act, but also dream; not only plan, but also believe.'

Anatole France

Introduction

Effective teaching ensures that where possible, the teaching and learning process is not only meaningful and authentic, but the assessment and reporting also reflects and captures authentic, accurate information for each individual student.

Effective assessment and reporting must be shared, discussed and owned by three key people: the student, the parent and the teacher. Traditional approaches to assessment and reporting are a limited and narrowed perspective in which assessment is something done 'to' a student—the student is basically passive in the process. A culture persists in many situations whereby the message conveyed is that assessment is simply a grade or number and that it can be accomplished by sitting a test every now and again.

Traditional views of assessment assume that:

- all children are ready and should be ready to learn the same thing at the same time in the same way

- one size fits all, despite the fact that culture, experience, exposure, opportunity and development all greatly impact on a student's ability and rate of learning

- testing is the most reliable way to ensure measurement of results that accurately reflect a student's current abilities

- collecting the same sample at the same time ensures a quality moderation of assessment. This has been proven wrong. Samples of work when the work is relevant is more likely to ensure authenticity (Wragg 1997).

Misunderstanding of the terms 'assessment' and 'reporting' can contribute to more superficial methods of testing that lack depth and meaning and do not reflect authentic observations or knowledge of children's learning.

- Assessment is a process of gathering and documenting information about the achievement, skills, abilities and personality variables of an individual, which informs teachers, parents and students about 'where to' next.

- Reporting involves collecting, compiling and sharing an overview of key information related to a specific issue or person. Reports may or may not make recommendations but in most cases they provide information about the way forward.

There are a number of factors that are integral to effective authentic assessment and reporting.

- Assessment should be viewed as an ongoing, continuous cycle of observing, collecting evidence, documenting and tracking where each student is looked at as an individual—where they were and where they are headed.

- Assessment is not the sole responsibility of the teacher or other authority within the school.

- Assessment includes self reflection, self assessment, peer assessment, parent input as well as teacher input and any other evidence that may be collected by teachers and students.

- Assessment and reporting involve a compilation of evidence over time, not once-off testing.

- Assessment and reporting are far more complex than just testing.

- Assessment must reflect authentic situations and examples that students can relate to and understand contextually.

- Meaningful assessment avoids multiple choice questions, tests and exams.

- Reporting must reflect a holistic picture of the student as an individual, a social being and a member of a community alongside aspects of learning and skill development.

- Assessment and reporting must be used to inform the next stage of teaching and learning for each student and avoid being used as once-off or intermittent tests simply to put a grade or number on a data sheet or report card.

In recent years, Western-based education systems have moved dramatically into standardised testing and in many cases this has distracted educators from continuing to ensure that ongoing, authentic and meaningful assessment and reporting is conducted. Unfortunately, while most educators understand the limitations, pressures and political aspects of collecting data based on prescribed national tests, they tend to preoccupy much of the discussion and time that teachers could otherwise be spending on ensuring that authentic assessment and reporting occurs. Discussions about progression points, grading, benchmarking, how to complete online tests scores and administer the tests is what tends to take up much of teachers' and schools' time and energy. This is without considering the time wasted for both children and teachers when 'teaching to the test'!

Unfortunately, it is difficult to imagine that national standardised testing will diminish in the near future. Therefore, the philosophy of the WLA—like most other approaches to teaching and learning—emphasises a number of elements that must be built into the assessment and reporting cycle within each classroom. This helps to broaden and deepen the information shared between teacher, student and parents, and also leads to better-informed teachers and students so that increasingly effective teaching and learning strategies can be used to cater for the needs and strengths of each student in their own learning cycle.

In this chapter we build on what meaningful assessment and reporting really is and how it can be achieved and disseminated to students, parents and the school. We also provide ideas for enhancing more holistic reporting strategies that reflect deeper achievements of students than just literacy and numeracy results.

Meaningful assessment and reporting

The WLA philosophy strongly recommends that in discussing meaningful assessment with parents and students, standardised testing be relegated to a secondary consideration. There are a number of other ways that meaningful assessment and reflection can be collected throughout the learning experience, such as:

- graphic organisers
- self assessment
- peer assessment
- rubric tables
- portfolios/journals
- teacher assessment
- samples of work
- oral reflections and presentations
- the expo
- ERP proposal forms
- the ERP projects themselves and the range of ways that students have demonstrated their understandings.

The following phrase underpins the meaningful assessment and reporting philosophy of the WLA:

> *The best assessment is where we can show where the child is now, where they were and where they are heading. Not where they are in relation to the rest of a class, school, community or world!*

Key aspects of WLA assessment include:

- the development of a portfolio that is shared, collated and added to by teacher, student and parents
- self assessment and self reflection
- peer assessment and feedback
- observation
- a variety of ways to assess and represent learning (for example, verbal, electronic, performance, construction, written)

- personalised records that capture learning and link to further goals (as described in Chapter 5).

These elements of WLA assessment are described in more detail below.

Reporting is about reflecting, evaluating and sharing information, and is much broader than simply a mid-year or end-of-year report that is sent home.

Key aspects of WLA reporting include:

- student-led conferencing
- student–teacher–parent interviews
- portfolios
- communication board
- expo
- individual student records
- state/territory/national reports.

These elements of WLA reporting are described in more detail later in this chapter.

We note that most states and territories require a written report at least every six months. These reports tend to emphasise grade levels and progression points and occasionally include tokenistic sections for students to contribute to. We recommend that reports of this nature are viewed by teachers, students and parents as simply state-imposed requirements, and do not constitute the major elements of meaningful assessment and reporting that continues all year.

WLA assessment

Portfolios

The development of portfolios has been the subject of much writing and many different professional development sessions in recent years. However, these discussions have mainly centred on types of portfolios rather than the *purpose* and *content* of portfolios. Identifying the purpose of a portfolio is necessary before any discussion can take place regarding what type it may be or what it may look like.

The WLA philosophy identifies that the purpose of a portfolio (either electronic or paper-based) is to inform and share information that is relevant, meaningful to the student and provides insights for teachers, students and parents in relation to:

- interests
- strengths
- challenges
- examples/samples
- comments/ideas
- reflections
- goals.

The WLA portfolio steps away from a predetermined list of dates for collecting predetermined samples of various bits and pieces. It is a dynamic, ongoing, collected range of work, learning, interactions, thoughts and reflections. The WLA portfolio includes the following:

- A general criteria list is established by teachers and students at the commencement of the year. Students are invited to offer ideas as to the sorts of information and examples of learning and experiences they would like included in their portfolios.

- Teachers then list the criteria, which may include samples and examples of:
  - writing in particular types
  - numeracy in a range of particular learning outcomes
  - designing and creating
  - personal reflection
  - social interactions

- subject focus learning intentions
- leadership and contribution
- rubrics
- peer assessment
- self assessment and reflections.

- The criteria list is discussed again with the students and pasted into the front cover of their portfolios as a checklist. Students are encouraged to contribute examples and ideas and add to the list whenever they wish.

- From time to time, teachers ensure that samples and evidence are being collated. Teachers as well as students can choose particular examples.

Portfolio ownership

Students should view the portfolio as their own. It is not stored or hidden away where the student cannot see it, own it or feel that they can contribute to it. The students collect evidence (as well as the teacher), collate it and are responsible for maintaining the portfolios with the direction of the teacher.

The portfolio audience

The portfolio is meant to be a living document that is available for parents, teachers and student to access, view and reflect on at any time. It can be taken home at intervals for discussion and sharing with parents; it can and should be used as part of parent–teacher–student interviews and to inform, guide and plan future learning. Teachers and students should refer to the portfolio when setting goals, revisiting where the student has moved to during a given period of time, and where or what they may be heading for or needing next.

Portfolio timelines

The portfolio is an ongoing tool for recording, documenting, reflecting and capturing some of each student's learning. It should be commenced at the beginning of a year and continued on throughout the year.

Self assessment and self reflection

Being able to reflect on one's own learning, behaviour, attitudes and interactions is an essential part of life. Traditional forms of assessment do not often provide opportunities for students to reflect on their own learning and, at times, this can engender a sense of fear, avoidance and suspicion, particularly for students who don't always perform well in test situations. For students who do perform well in such tests, they become used to external (extrinsic) reinforcement of themselves as a learner or performer, rather than with an intrinsic sense of what their learning strengths and challenges might be.

A learning environment that denies authentic opportunities for regular reflection and self assessment perpetuates a belief that assessment is done 'to you', rather than as a means to identify future directions, and to gain ideas of where you currently are in terms of strengths, extension needs and further assistance. It sends a message that students are not empowered to assess themselves and take responsibility for some of their learning.

Examples and ideas

- being the focus student (reflecting and sharing with class on ERPs, timelines, research skills, information gained, organisation skills)
- completion of a rubric
- portfolio entries, written reflections
- identifying needs and participating in compulsory and optional clinic groups
- reporting and sharing at the expo.

Peer assessment and feedback

Life, careers and learning are most commonly shared alongside others. Gaining perspectives, interactions, feedback and opinions from others is an important part of working and living a successful life. It is not easy for adults—let alone children—to share ideas, and receive feedback and opinions about themselves or their learning. However, it is important that a community such as a classroom is a safe place that creates a culture of positive, honest and productive interactions where students are encouraged to seek, receive and give feedback to and from their peers. Creating this culture of shared opinions, feedback and assessment takes modelling, time and trust.

Suggestions and ideas

- facilitating reflection between students during weekly class meeting

- questions and responses from peers when reporting back and sharing information about ERPs

- 1:1 dialogue where each student shares with their peer something they have noticed is a strength in learning or general attributes, attitudes

- 1:1 dialogue where each student contributes an idea or strategy that may assist or support a specific challenge or need, or where additional ideas are needed or asked for.

Observation

Through daily interactions with students, teachers are observing and making mental notes, noticing aspects of learning and behaviour and how students interact and socialise with others. Often we take these mental notes for granted. These observations are in fact an important, authentic aspect of assessment and worth capturing in some ways at various times.

Some teachers make extra notes on individual record sheets when children are focus students. Some teachers make a few notes on the daily record sheet. Some teachers ensure that a few extra notes have been recorded, or photos taken of each student over the fortnight.

Observation during each day is one of the most powerful and dynamic ways to assess learning and progress. Students are often at their most natural when they think they are not being 'tested' and it is during ordinary daily work and learning that teachers can gain great insights into students and their learning behaviours.

A variety of ways to represent and assess learning

Traditionally, testing and assessment generally has depended largely on the need to write responses and answers. Unless certain children were identified as having specific learning needs, this assumption was always upheld for the majority of students.

While some aspects of literacy do require written responses and some learning requires written information, there has been a lack of broader and wider options for students who, for example, may know certain information and could verbally convey it effectively and correctly but their handwriting or other writing issues hamper and misrepresent what they actually know.

An important feature of the WLA is the opportunity to ensure that students have a wide range of ways in which they can reflect their learning, understandings and skills. The ERP is an example of how assessed work does not always have to be in written form. Certainly the project proposal needs to be completed, but for students who find handwriting difficult and may disengage from the process, this could be typed rather than handwritten.

Providing a range of options (such as a verbal report, a PowerPoint presentation, a performance, or a music composition) in which assessment can be made helps ensure that the teacher does not inadvertently test or assess the wrong thing (i.e., testing the handwriting rather than the actual learning that has taken place).

Table 6.1 provides an example of a rubric which can be used to assess students' learning. This is also included on the CD.

WLA reporting

Student-led conferencing

Sharing between the teacher and a focus student is a powerful way in which the teacher can encourage the student to reflect and report on their own learning. Through discussing their ERP or other aspects of their learning, the student is able—along

Table 6.1 Example of an assessment rubric

ERP Assessment Guide Grades 5–6

the Walker Learning Approach — DEVELOPMENTALLY APPROPRIATE PRACTICE

	Extremely high level of learning	High level of learning	Satisfactory	Needs to work much harder
Proposal preparation, consideration and completion	• Completes proposal independently with considerable detail • Locates information from a wide range of sources and adjusts search as new information is found • Independently makes clear links between set criteria and area of interest	• Able to complete proposal independently • Locates information from a wide range of sources • Identifies some links between set criteria and area of interest	• Able to complete proposal with a little support • Able to locate information from some sources • Contributes ideas to link set criteria to own interests	• More effort is required when completing proposal • Extra support and ideas required to complete proposal • Has difficulty locating information from possible sources
Timeline	• Uses time very well • Completes work ahead of schedule	• Completes work on time • Monitors and manages work habits and schedule well	• Completes most work on time • Monitors schedule reasonably well	• More attention to timelines required • More attention to monitoring own progress required
Student-led conference	• Well prepared to lead conference • Provides clear, detailed and logical information on progress	• Well prepared to lead conference • Provides clear and accurate information on progress	• Able to lead conference and explain current progress with ERP	• Information and progress must be clear • More focus required during conference
Personal goals	• Thoughtful and appropriate choice of personal goals	• Able to set personal goals independently	• Able to set personal goals with little support	• Less teacher support should be used in setting personal goals
Project goals and intentions achieved	• All project goals have been achieved and exceeded • Able to elaborate on goals, intentions and understanding of ERP	• All project goals have been achieved • Able to articulate project goals and intentions and carefully monitor these throughout ERP	• Nearly all project goals are completed • Needs a little support to articulate or demonstrate achievement of goals	• More attention to demonstrating evidence of achieving project goals required
Peer assessment	• Demonstrates an ability to constructively review and integrate feedback from peers	• Attentive to feedback from peers and provides thoughtful review	• Listens and responds positively to feedback	• Work towards better listening and reviewing of peer feedback
ERP artefact artwork	• Artwork demonstrates a unique level of originality • Demonstrates thoughtful and detailed links to ERP focus	• Artwork shows original and creative skills • Links to ERP focus are clear and related	• Artwork is creative and shows some link to ERP focus	• More evidence of original thought required for artwork piece • Clearer relationship required between artwork and ERP focus

Engagement Matters © Kathy Walker and Shona Bass 2011

with the teacher's direction—to consolidate and identify where they may need to head next, what aspects of their learning they need to focus more on and what their current strengths are.

Student–teacher–parent interviews

Many schools now include students as an integral part of the parent–teacher interview. The WLA recommends this approach in the majority of circumstances. This three-way discussion builds strong links between home and school and encourages open communication and sharing from all perspectives.

It is very powerful and meaningful for parents to have their own children talk them through their learning; to share more of their portfolios, ERPs, individual record files and other samples of their learning. It is interesting for teachers to note what aspects of the learning students choose to share at these meetings.

The parent–teacher–student interview demonstrates that there are no secrets in learning and teaching. It provides empowerment and engagement for students to take some ownership and responsibility for their learning and to share it with their parents in a formal situation.

Portfolios

As mentioned in the assessment and documentation parts of the chapter, portfolios are an authentic way of capturing key events, skills and learning experiences across a wide range of areas that reflect and represent some of the students' learning.

Communication board

This is a means of communicating (or reporting) to parents and students some of the learning that is taking place. It provides opportunities for discussion at home about some of the learning intentions and experiences that are being provided and the students are participating in.

The expo

The expo provides an additional, exciting way for students to report back, to share their reflections and to be accountable to their proposal and their learning. The expo provides opportunities for students to present and share verbally what and how they have learned, through a range of different mediums, such as exhibitions, artefacts, constructions and multimedia.

Individual student records

The individual student record provides the opportunity for teachers to develop a continuous meaningful assessment of all aspects of students' development and learning. Entries are made when the students are focus students and at other times when the student has demonstrated the acquisition of skills and knowledge. The individual student records are electronically based and each student has a file. We recommend that sections of this reporting are copied and pasted into the students' school reports.

The state/territory/national report

These reports are just one other way in which some of the learning is captured and documented. Ideally, the report would emphasise the progress of the individual measured mostly against their own journey rather than attempting to place them in a narrow grade or measurement against a cohort or nation.

Other issues related to assessment and reporting

Many teachers struggle with how to report on what seem to be so many different outcomes in so many content-based subjects. Questions include, 'How can we fit everything in?' and 'How can we assess against every outcome?' There is often an assumption in these questions that somehow in the past, we were able to test and assess every student in authentic ways against every single outcome, and that the assessment was accurate. The reality about meaningful assessment and reporting is that it is impossible to truly assess every child against every outcome.

What we can do, and what the WLA philosophy encourages and supports teachers in doing, is to ensure that through the range of assessment tools (self assessment, peer assessment, daily reflections, portfolio development, ERPs and any other assessment that is used by the school), a richer and wider range of meaningful assessment will be reflected. Being able to recite pieces of information for testing purposes does not equate to meaningful assessment, nor does regurgitated information truly reflect internalised, deep learning and understandings.

Therefore, in trying to capture a grade level or progression point, assessment will always eventually rest with the subjective evaluation of a teacher. The more a teacher knows a student holistically, the more likely it is that an accurate grade level can be predicted and relied on than when dealing only with a test situation.

In the current political climate of education, it is unlikely that standardised testing will disappear. Therefore, it is imperative that educators continue to maximise opportunities to provide a wide range of student-empowered assessment and reporting which broadens and deepens everyone's understanding, and focus on what effective and important assessment should be as part of the teaching–learning cycle.

Summary

Assessment and reporting are an integral and important aspect of learning. A holistic range of assessment and reporting strategies ensures that:

- students are empowered to identify some of their own learning

- students take greater responsibility for themselves

- reflection and evaluation are developed, which are critical abilities throughout life in relation to careers, future study and relationships.

Focusing on the broader and richer aspects of assessment and reporting also conveys powerful messages to students and parents:

- Meaningful assessment is not about comparison with the rest of the world.

- The progress and journey of each individual needs to be carefully reflected in a wide range of assessment and reporting opportunities.

Whole class experiences

Tuning in and reflection time

Tuning in and reflection time begin and end each day. These times are conducted as a conversation between the focus students and the rest of the class. There are three focus students each day.

The teacher models and scaffolds the learning intentions during tuning in and reflection.

Class meeting

Class meetings always have a leader, agenda and minute-taker. These provide opportunities for student leadership and practice in running meetings. The emphasis should be on global and community events rather than classroom rules or behaviour issues.

Learning environment/classroom set-up

Students take a lead role in setting up their learning environment. This is part of ownership of their learning. The learning area should include chairs, tables, sofas, break-out spaces, cushions and the communication board. The space provides opportunities for students to work alone, together and in small groups.

Clinic groups (compulsory and optional)

Compulsory clinic group

A clinic group is designed for small group leadership, learning and collaboration. Clinic groups can be based on numeracy, literacy, skills or technology, or any other interest initiated by teachers, parents and students. They can also be taught by teachers, students, parents, or other members of the community.

Optional clinic group

These encourage children to opt into groups for learning and provide opportunities for students, parents and others to lead groups, to have practice in decision-making and to participate in leading, learning and working collaboratively in small groups.

Examples of optional clinic groups lead by students:

i. crystal formation and links to geology

ii. strategies when playing chess.

Examples of optional clinic groups lead by teachers:
i. taking learning outdoors; making an outdoor weaving loom
ii. making clay tablets.

Clinic groups provide an emphasis on personalised learning alongside students working together in all areas of curriculum.

Education research projects

Student-led conference

Students are encouraged to talk about their proposal, justify their ideas and interests and how they link to learning intentions. This is done 1:1 with the teacher, in clinic groups and in whole-group discussions.

Education research projects

EPRs encourage a wide range of technologies and methods of production. They include an extensive range of strategies, such as videos, documentaries, poetry, song writing, claymation, animation, stories, diorama, dance choreography, artwork, music production, etc.

Students must include rationale as to why and how they wish to produce a particular project in a specific way.

The following images are examples of ERP projects by students whose focus area was the arts. The projects were required to meet the following outcomes:

- identify techniques, skills and aspects of an artist's work
- use arts elements, skills, techniques and processes to create and present an original artwork
- convey a message or emotion to the intended audience through the artwork.

Fancy fruitcake

Julia appreciates the artistic elements in preparing special foods and she has always wanted to attempt to make and decorate a cake.

Julia used many cake decorating books for inspiration and settled on a cake with patterned icing with a flower. Julia enlisted the skills of Miss Kenna, a student teacher who decorates cakes as a hobby.

The final product was a very tempting dessert and Julia says it tasted delicious!

Michael Jackson

Zane's focus artist is Michael Jackson. Zane has been a passionate Michael Jackson fan since the first time he saw the Thriller music video. Zane believes that Michael Jackson was an all-round talented performer.

Zane studied Jackson's choreography and created a compilation of his signature moves, including the 'moonwalk', 'circle slide' and 'kick'. He choreographed his own dance based on these moves and performed to an audience of his peers.

Zane intended to transfer the energy and emotion that dancing can produce to his audience.

The rainbow serpent

Lavina's painting is inspired by her Indigenous Australian heritage. Lavina appreciates traditional art as well as the colours and techniques used in modern Aboriginal Australian art.

Lavina's focus artist is Natalie Bateman. Bateman is an Aboriginal Yuin artist and shares Lavina's interest in modern and abstract art. She blends traditional techniques—such as using echidna quills—with contemporary designs.

Lavina has used bright colours in her painting to make her audience feel happy and captivated.

Rey Mysterio mask

Krona is an avid fan of wrestling, so he used this as a basis for his arts ERP. Krona loves the masks that wrestler Rey Mysterio wears and decided to create one similar.

Krona chose to make a mask from papier-mâché as his investigations into mask-making suggested that this was one of the best methods to use when creating a mask for the first time.

Krona's intended audience is boys and teenagers. He hopes to make them feel the excitement of wrestling through his mask design.

Sports car design

George has a passion for sports cars and he is impressed with their speed and design. He was keen to try his hand at designing his own sports car for his ERP.

George's focus artist is Chip Foose, a sports car designer who has been creating designs since he was seven years old. Features of Foose's designs are clean lines, attention to detail and cars that people will stop and take notice of. George tried to keep these features in mind when he created his own designs.

George's intended audience is car manufacturers such as Ferrari and Lamborghini.

The expo

Each term in Week 7 or 8, an expo is held where students organise, prepare and present their ERPs individually for parents and the school and wider community. The emphasis is on the proposal and learning, not just the actual project.

Communication board

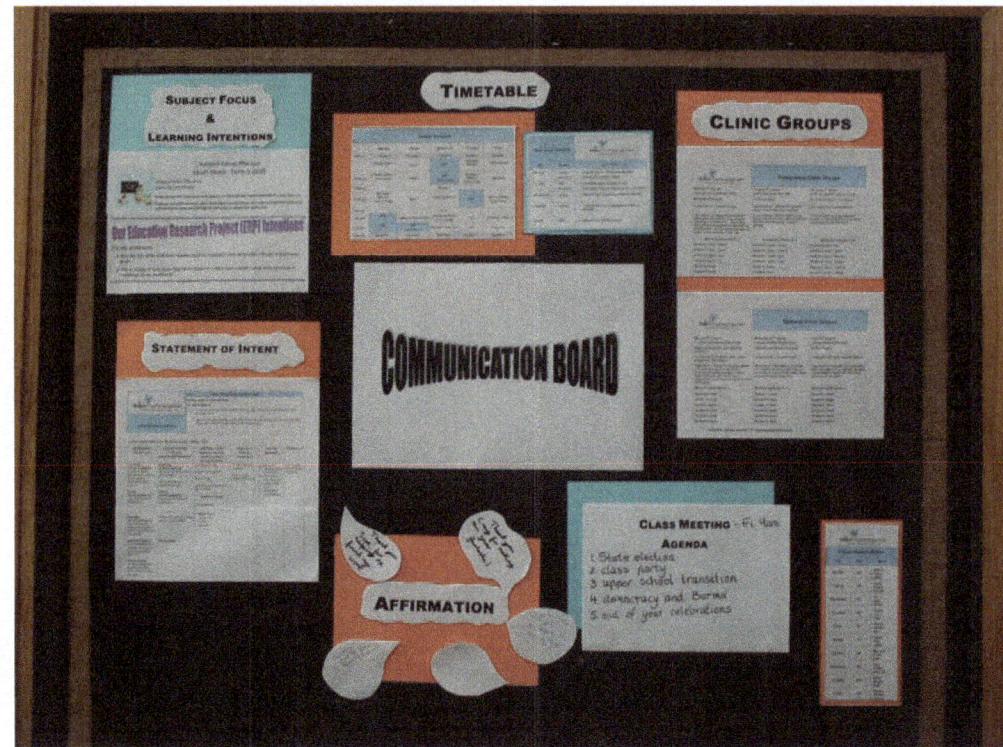

The communication board

The communication board is a vital part of the approach. The board is managed by the teacher and students. It is considered a shared conduit for communication. The following information is displayed on the board: subject focus and learning intentions, term timetable, statement of intent, clinic group timetable, clinic group sign-up forms, class meeting agenda, focus student roster, and affirmation section.

The communication board

Students 'check in' with the communication board each day to organise their diaries and to check for clinic groups, notices, or to add to the class meeting agenda.

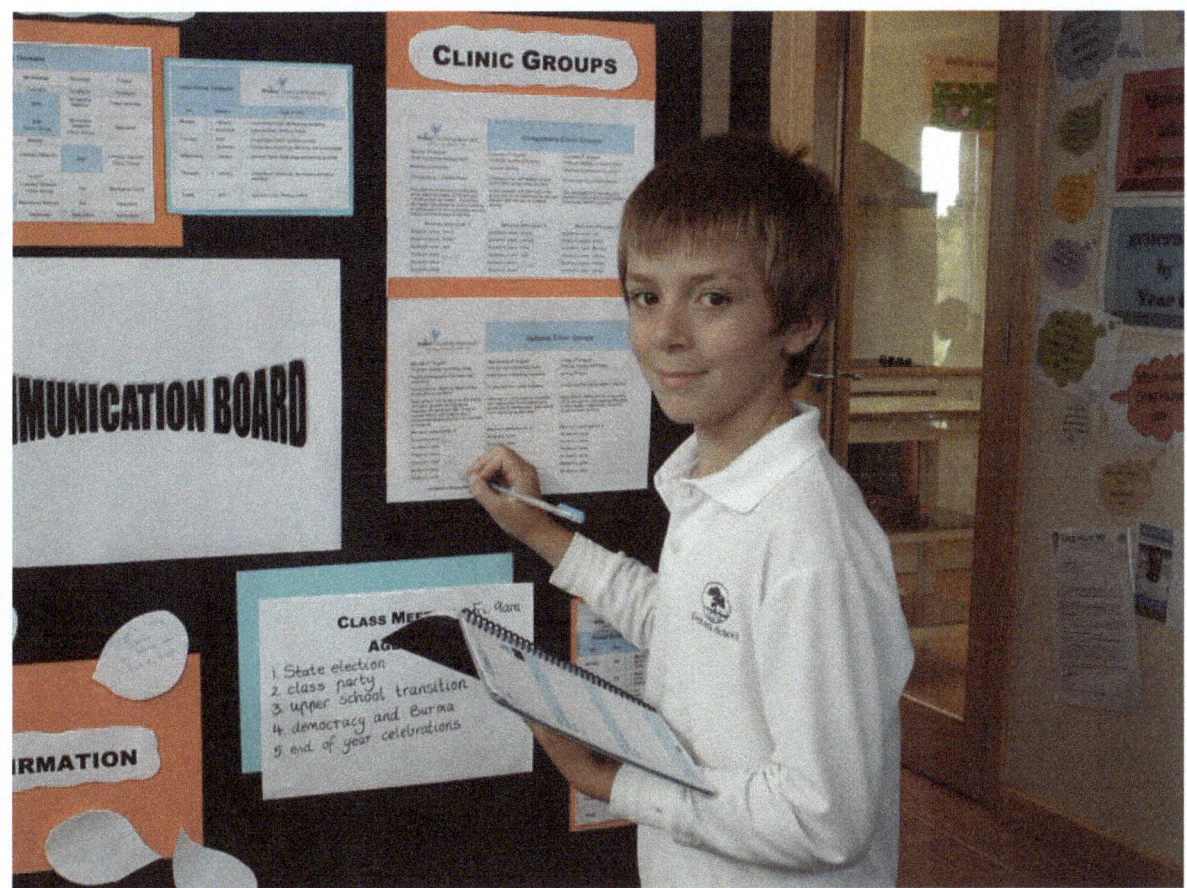

Clinic group sign-up forms

Students are encouraged to sign up for optional clinic groups in order to promote independence, organisational skills and planning.

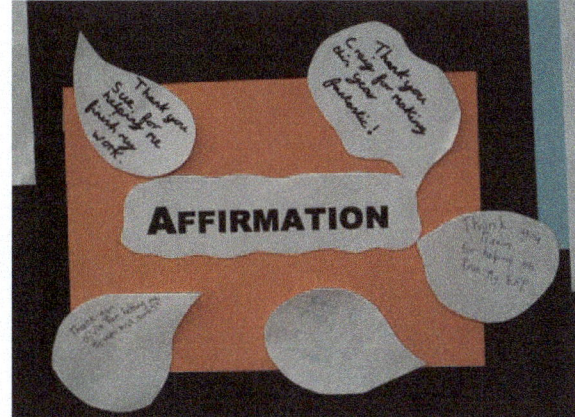

Affirmation

Students are encouraged to publically interact with each other and consciously provide appropriate positive acknowledgements.

Class meeting

Students are encouraged to list issues for discussion each week.

Chapter 7

Case studies

'Your vision will become clear only when you look into your heart. Who looks outside, dreams. Who looks inside, awakens.'

Carl Jung

Introduction

This chapter provides some real life examples of the development of ERP proposals and how teachers and students can work together during ERP times. It also unpacks in detail the progression, support and understanding the teacher needs to bring to students to ensure the successful implementation of the ERP. Many students will find the processes and the deep thinking required for the ERP new and challenging. Teachers should not interpret this initial difficulty as ERPs being too hard or beyond the students, and should not simplify the proposals and contracts or reduce expectations. The teacher must support, demonstrate and model the skills and understandings for the students in appropriately sequenced teaching sessions (1:1; 1:small group and 1:whole class). This chapter will help guide the teacher on how to best approach this task.

Developing the ERP proposal

It is important to use the ERP proposal form as a formal teaching tool. The proposal form is not designed for students to work through on their own; as discussed in Chapter 3, developing the skills and understandings to complete the proposal is a major part of the teaching and learning process. It requires deep thinking, planning, reflection and personalising learning. The examples used in the case studies demonstrate how ERPs are formed through children's interests and then linked back into learning intentions. We also use examples to demonstrate how to use the ERP proposal form as a working document with students.

Case study A unpacks how the teacher works from the planning documents to model and support the students to develop their ERP proposal related to economics. Case studies B and C have been purposely presented to demonstrate how the same student interest (Australian Rules football) can be applied to two different subject themes (health and Australian history).

Case study A

The subject focus for the term is economics. The teaching team will have planned and mapped out (i) the key learning intentions from the subject focus outcomes in the framework, and (ii) what they aim to achieve for the first six sessions of the ERP (as described below).

Term 3 Subject Focus: Economics

Key learning intentions: As identified by teaching team in Grade 5 and from subject focus outcomes in framework.

For students to:

- *demonstrate and describe understanding of earning, budgeting and saving*

- *demonstrate and represent aspects of advertising, marketing and planning*

- *gain understanding of the relationship between work, career and income.*

During the first 6 sessions of ERP time, the teacher is aiming to achieve:

- identification of the students' authentic interests

- introduction to and immersion of information about learning intentions and subject focus

- commencing developing proposals with students in whole, small and individual sessions

- information sharing of general facts and concepts.

In addition, throughout the remainder of the term, incursions, excursions and input sessions will continue.

The following sections map out how the teacher introduces the ERP to the students in the first week, typical examples of student–teacher discussions, the development of the ERP over subsequent weeks and examples of clinic groups.

ERP Session 1: Week 1 summary

- General discussion by teacher of holidays, children's current interests.

- Introduction to term subject focus (only *after* the general discussion): 'This term our subject focus is economics. Does anyone know what that is or means?' General discussion.

- Then, 'Our first challenge is to think about how your current interests may be able to meet our key learning intentions in economics and what type of project you might be interested in. Let me show you and talk about what the key learning intentions under economics are …'

These are then shown, described and unpacked initially and then continue to be unpacked with examples throughout the term.

Example of student–teacher discussions

- 'Over the term we will be taking you to some shops, having someone visit us here in class to talk about their job at McDonald's, and giving you lots of other information about economics. We have some planned activities to help you gain understanding about these learning intentions.'

- 'These discussions might help you link your interest to our subject focus outcomes.'

A general brainstorm of students' initial interests as identified in the general discussion is compiled and the teacher models and gives examples of how some of the interests may or may not link. For example:

- Child A says their current interest is their new shoes, which are Nike brand. This is an easy interest to link into a project and to meet outcomes related to marketing, advertising and earning.

- Child B says their current interest is football. This might also be linked to advertising, marketing, brands, income and sponsors.

Some children at this point may have no clearly defined interest or an interest that seems impossible or challenging to link. This is OK in the preliminary stages. The immersion phase of excursions, visits, input and activities from the teacher and examples and ideas from other students will help these students to eventually find a project interest. This is part of learning: having to think, reject some ideas, try to make links and share ideas with peers.

Subsequent weeks/ERP sessions

Remember, the aim is not to make the child fit the subject—it is to make the subject fit the child! That is, we are trying to 'hook the children in' through their authentic interests that can then be linked to and meet the learning intentions.

During the first 2–3 weeks particularly, the teacher will provide lots of examples, exposure, input and information to help students gain understanding related to the subject focus outcomes. It is now that the proposal forms are commenced—the important point here is that the proposal is developed over time. The proposal process advances as the students gain more understanding, unpack their own ideas and negotiate with the teacher.

Examples of how to work with students on their proposal forms

Whole group discussions

The teacher might say:

- 'Let's work through the first few sections of the proposal form together.'

- 'What are our focus and learning intentions?'

- 'What are you each hoping to find out about your interest and how does it link to our learning intentions?'

- 'What literacy and numeracy might we add in?'

In small groups or clinic groups

- 'How might you like to represent and demonstrate your learning and project?'

The idea here is that teachers work their way through the proposal form in sections, helping students to think, plan and identify their ideas and learning. This process will occur over a number of sessions.

> **Student A: Proposal on economics and Nike shoes (initial draft)**
>
> *Subject focus:* Economics, Grade 5
>
> *Key learning intentions:*
>
> For students to:
> - demonstrate and describe understanding of earning, budgeting and saving
> - demonstrate and represent aspects of advertising, marketing and planning
> - gain understanding of the relationship between work, career and income.
>
> *My interest:* Nike shoes
>
> *How it links to subject focus outcomes:* I will use my interest in Nike shoes to show how I could market and advertise them.
> - I could research how much they cost to make and how much they are sold for.
> - I could do a survey of students to see how many like Nike shoes and how many students don't.
>
> *My project will include:*
> - A poster for advertising which will include costs, information and how many countries they are sold in.
> - A short video about my Nike shoes.
>
> *Numeracy component:* Collecting data through a survey of students
>
> *Literacy component:* To write a short persuasive piece on why people should buy Nike brand.
>
> *Note:* The numeracy and literacy components can either be personalised and therefore slightly different for each student or linked to specific literacy and numeracy skills currently a focus throughout the term. (This is an example of a component set by teacher for all students.)
>
> *My current strengths:* Using video and photography, using computers.
>
> *My challenge:* To keep to my timeline of 6 weeks because I often don't stay on task.
>
> *Work individual/team:* I would like to work on my own.
>
> *Note:* If two students share an interest and the teacher is happy for them to work on a combined project this is OK. However, it is important to note that each student must complete their own proposal form. This ensures each student is personalising their learning, skills and needs within the project.

Once each student has identified their key interest and project brief, they can commence the initial stages of their project. They don't need to have completed the entire form before they begin.

The proposal form is a work in progress alongside the student's work on their actual project. However, it is anticipated that the major elements of each proposal could be signed off and finalised by the end of sessions 6 and 7.

What does each ERP session look like?

- Perhaps a whole group discussion, general sharing from focus children or others about their project and learning.

- Input from teacher, excursion/incursion activities planned by teacher.

- Information sharing by teacher. Certain facts or figures that are important for students to know.

- Clinic groups or one-on-one student conferencing for teacher to work alongside students.

- Students have time to work on their project.

Students do not need to spend lots of time on computers or accessing books about Nike. Some information will be required, but the main work of the student is to match their interest to demonstrate learning intentions and complete their project.

The key focus is always bringing students back to the learning intentions. For example, teacher questions might include:

- 'How is your project meeting the learning intentions?'
- 'What have you learned about marketing through this project?'

Remember: The student isn't 'doing' a project about Nike: they are simply using their interest in Nike as a catalyst to demonstrate how they can meet and understand the key learning intentions required for the term in economics.

Case studies B and C

Case studies B and C have been purposely presented to demonstrate how the same student interest (Australian Rules football) can be applied to two different subject themes (health and Australian history).

Student B: Proposal on health and Australian Rules football (initial draft)

Subject focus: Health, Grade 3

Key learning intentions:

For students to:
- *demonstrate awareness and understanding of the differences between healthy and unhealthy foods*
- *demonstrate and describe the importance of physical fitness as part of a healthy lifestyle*
- *consider and identify some aspects of an unhealthy lifestyle.*

My interest: Australian Rules football

How it links to subject focus outcomes:
- *I will use my interest in Aussie rules footy to show how footballers have to train and what they eat and drink to stay fit.*
- *I will give some examples of what happens when some football players take too much alcohol and drugs and how it hurts their health and family.*

My project will include:
- *A PowerPoint presentation of information about training programs for football players and how this keeps them fit.*
- *A collage construction of parts of the body needed for fitness and health in a football player.*

Numeracy component: *I will record the heights and weights of football players who play for Essendon Football Club. I will report the average height for each position (backs, forwards, rucks and midfield) and identify which playing positions have the tallest and shortest players.*

Literacy component: *I will produce my PowerPoint file with subheadings, graphs and as a factual presentation.*

Note: The numeracy and literacy components can either be personalised and therefore slightly different for each student or linked to specific literacy and numeracy skills currently a focus throughout the term. (This is an example of a component set by teacher for all students.)

My current strengths: Knowledge of football, playing football and using the computer.

My challenge: *To organise my PowerPoint presentation in ways that are different from the last one I presented, and to include the numeracy section.*

Student C: Proposal on history and Australian Rules football (initial draft)

Subject focus: Australian history, Grades 5–6

Key learning intentions:

For students to:
- demonstrate awareness and understanding of early immigration and the history and impact of diversity in Australia in the mid 1850s and beyond
- demonstrate and describe some key components of early white settlement in Australia.

My interest: Australian Rules football

How it links to subject focus outcomes:
- I will use my interest in Aussie rules footy to show how different groups from other parts of the world brought their own sport and interests to Australia and how they are similar or different from Aussie rules.
- I will find out when Aussie rules football started and how it was invented and who invented it.
- I will find out if our indigenous people played any sports or football and what happened after white settlement.

My project will include:
- I will write a song with music about when white people arrived in Australia and the sport they played.
- I will pretend to be a reporter and will interview some teachers about what they know about the types of groups that came to Australia in the mid 1800s. I will film this and make it into a documentary.

Numeracy component: I will draw a timeline that lists when different groups arrived in Australia and when on the timeline Aussie rules football started.

Literacy component: My documentary will have a script of questions.

Note: The numeracy and literacy components can either be personalised and therefore slightly different for each student or linked to specific literacy and numeracy skills currently a focus throughout the term. (This is an example of a component set by teacher for all students.)

My current strengths: Knowledge of football and music.

My challenge: To work out when Aussie rules football started in Australia and what types of sport indigenous people played before white people arrived.

Summary

Developing the ERP proposal

- Start with students' authentic interests and try to work from there.

- Ensure teachers and students are clear about the learning intentions.

- Never use the term 'topic' or the expression, 'This term we are doing …' Instead, 'This term our subject focus is … and our main learning intentions are …'

- Ensure the student has chosen an interest that will enable them to:

  - access enough information

  - link to the learning intentions

  - extend their knowledge in their own interest, as well as scaffold them into meeting the learning intentions required.

Final points of reassurance

- If the student chooses an interest that you really cannot link in a meaningful way, you are allowed to say 'no' and move them into their next idea. You as the teacher are also able to make suggestions and give input into their choice. The key point, however, is that we are attempting to help students engage meaningfully through their own authentic interests.

- If a student wants to choose the same interest each term, use your discretion and knowledge of the student. Some students may work productively and in a highly engaged manner through the same interest. The proposal form will ensure different outcomes, scope and project requirements. Other students may need you to move them onto a new interest. Your knowledge of each student will help you to make the decision.

Conservation of Forest

CONTROL POPULATION
CONSERVATION OF FOREST
SAVE TIGER
SOIL EROSION
SAVE RHINO
PREVENT
STOP POLLUTION

Chapter 8

Troubleshooting and frequently asked questions

In this chapter we address the most frequently asked questions, comments and queries that have come up since we started implementing the WLA Grades 3–6 program. In most cases we will address these questions with a short response and where possible we will refer the reader back to specific relevant sections in the book.

Can one teacher implement the approach when the rest of the team or leadership don't want to?

There are a number of points here. Generally, as discussed in Chapter 1, a school or team either believes in something or doesn't, and the teaching and learning needs to reflect a consistent and shared philosophy and approach. It is desirable for the school or at least the teaching team to provide a consistent message to parents in how the teaching and learning needs to look (refer to Chapter 3).

It is not recommended that one teacher tries to implement the WLA in isolation from the rest of the school. This can be a lonely experience, placing pressure on the one teacher who attempts to 'go it alone' and potentially leading to the view that they are 'different', impairing the results of the program. It can also be difficult to explain to prospective parents why one classroom looks different from the rest.

Can we start straight away?

Some very enthusiastic teachers wish to start implementing the WLA immediately after reading the book or attending an introductory session. As much as we encourage teachers to have a go and to be excited about using the approach, it is very important that time, reflection, mentoring, preparation of the classroom and some understanding of the WLA are explored first. Leadership needs to be consulted, other team members may need to be updated or attend an introductory session and time needs to be set aside for further practical support before commencement.

The trap in launching enthusiastically into the WLA without appropriate time, preparation and mentoring is that the integrity and rigour of the approach is not achieved, teachers, students and parents become disgruntled and confused and teachers end up heading down a path that is not consistent with the core elements of the approach.

As discussed in Chapter 3, we recommend at least a six-month lead time with some mentoring during those six months so the team can prepare appropriately.

How will we explain it to the parents who may think it's just 'play' or that we have stopped teaching?

The school must provide a parent information session at least once a year about the teaching and learning that occurs in the school. This is a proactive approach and provides a shared set of strategies and beliefs which help parents understand that their children are still being taught the basic skills in literacy and numeracy along with other important concepts and life skills.

Inviting parents to regularly familiarise themselves with the documents on the communication board (see Chapter 2) helps to share the philosophy and substantiate the learning that is occurring. Parents need to have a basic understanding of the key documents such as the SOI, ERP, portfolio and the term subject focus (see Chapters 2, 3, 4 and 5). Displaying photos of learning in all subject areas with learning intentions clearly stated where they can be viewed and accessed also helps parents to appreciate and feel comfortable with the WLA.

Providing parents with regular updates of individual records, photos and information about the child either through electronic forms, journals, portfolios or parent–teacher–student interviews also helps parents understand and embrace the WLA.

How do we deal with people in authority who do not understand the approach and believe it may compromise literacy or numeracy?

Decision-makers outside of the school community need to be informed and up to date with best practice in teaching and learning and the skills that students need to succeed in the future. Understanding the philosophy and rigour of the WLA of course leads to an appreciation that literacy and numeracy are still taught formally each day alongside even more literacy and numeracy experiences through clinic groups, whole group instruction and the ERPs.

It is recommended that people in decision-making positions attend one of the WLA introductory sessions or are encouraged to meet with us so that they can be given full and accurate information about the WLA in order to discourage assumptions, misunderstandings or misinterpretations.

How will we cover the content in the framework and meet all outcomes?

The ERP model provides a systematic approach to ensuring that each term there is one subject area focus, such as history, health, society and environment (refer to Chapter 4). Schools establish a system that ensures that all subject areas are a focus at some stage over a one- or two-year cycle (depending on how each school wishes to set specific subject foci each term). Key learning intentions are still set and assessed as described in Chapter 4.

Literacy and numeracy are still taught each day and increased opportunities are provided for additional personalised literacy and numeracy through the clinic groups.

What is the difference between an ERP 'subject focus' and a 'topic' from other inquiry models?

This is clarified in Chapter 4 which details how the ERPs are implemented. The key differences include:

- A subject focus is broader than a traditional topic.

- A subject focus identifies key learning intentions based on government frameworks.

- A subject focus does not lock students into narrow or teacher-directed topics such as 'the gold rush' or 'planets'. It encourages students to seek an area of interest that is meaningful and engaging to them. Learning intentions and expectations based on the subject focus outcomes are then set by the teacher through the ERP process.

- A subject focus and ERP concentrates on skills, research and broad exposure to a range of concepts or content. They reconceptualise the emphasis away from starting with the *topic* ('We are doing the gold rush'), to starting with the *interests of the children* and moving towards the learning objectives. The starting points are at opposite ends of the spectrum.

- ERPs do not start with the same key understandings for all students. The WLA personalises key understandings based on the interests and ERP of each student. The teacher then audits these alongside learning intentions.

- In its simplest form, the ERP starts with the child's interest and the learning intentions from a broad subject area, rather than starting with a narrow predetermined topic.

How do we ensure that the 'data' is maintained?

Results, information and data will all continue to be collected, audited and evaluated as they always have been. As discussed in Chapter 6, results and monitoring of students' learning is more extensive, authentic and broad in the WLA than in traditional teaching methods.

The research results show that when the WLA is implemented with integrity and rigour, the data collected is enhanced and certainly not compromised. Our evidence reflects improvement in all areas of learning including social skills, research skills, independence as well as literacy and numeracy (Walker 2009).

Can the WLA be implemented without appropriate professional development and mentoring?

The short answer is no. Ongoing mentoring and professional development ensures that teachers are supported and provided with suggestions and strategies as they implement the WLA over the first 1–2 years and that teachers have the opportunity to debrief, reflect and evaluate how they are going with professionals expert in the approach.

As with any teaching and learning approach, shared understandings across the team and school, support from leadership, ongoing assistance with ideas and strategies, and expert and informed encouragement from the designers and researchers of the WLA ensure not only that the integrity of the program is preserved, but that the quality of teaching and learning within the school is enhanced.

Will it cost much to implement the WLA? Is it expensive to resource?

The WLA does not require an expensive outlay or large budget. It is actually cheaper to resource the Grades 3–6 approach than it is for the first three years of investigations. The classroom set-up (as described in Chapter 4) may be a little different, and some additional resources of clay, etc. will be accessed. But in general, the cost of resources is no different from a regular classroom.

The real costs that must be kept in mind when planning a budget for the WLA are those associated with mentoring and professional development rather than for lots of resources. It is important that schools allocate a budget to ensure continued professional development and mentoring.

How will we provide resources for all the different projects?

ERPs do not necessarily require students to be accessing lots of 'information' (see Chapter 4). One of the aims of the WLA is to shift students away from the mentality of simply gathering facts and figures, or cutting and pasting information. Rather, while teachers will obviously provide a range of resources and information for students based on the focus subject and key learning intentions, the students are encouraged to construct, explore, express and produce a range of different ways to demonstrate that they have met the intentions. If there are certain facts and figures of a general nature related to the intentions, we recommend teachers simply share this information at the outset.

If some students choose a project that seems impossible to complete, then the teacher can redirect the student to think of another project that will make it easier to access information.

What about the child who doesn't know what or how to choose their project?

There will always be children who are not able to identify an appropriate project interest. The immersion phase early in each term aims to help students gather ideas and spark interests in new experiences and excursions. Tuning in time each morning allows focus students to model appropriate project choices for their peers (see Chapter 2).

If there are students who are still not able to identify an interest for their ERP, the teacher can help direct them to a particular interest.

How can students have the skills to identify projects and interests, and work on individual or small group projects?

Teachers still need to teach and instruct. For example, the ERP proposal needs to be talked through and modelled with students, especially in the first term of implementation. It should not be assumed that because students are provided with greater freedom to choose areas of interest, to attend clinic groups and to contribute more authentically to their own learning environment, that teachers stop instructing. Formal instruction and modelling will always be necessary and are an important part of the WLA.

ERP sessions will often include and involve formal modelling and instruction on how to set a timeline, how to organise the project and how to access information.

How do Grade 3 students adapt and work this way as they move from Grade 2?

Some children will be ready to make the progression and move into ERPs. Some children moving into Grade 3 will still reflect a maturity level that is more at a Grade 2 or 1 level. We recommend a number of strategies to assist children as they make the significant move from Grade 2 to ensure a smooth and enjoyable transition into Grade 3.

- Term 1 may be a combination of investigations and mini ERPs.

- During the course of Grade 3, some children will continue to need investigations or mini projects rather than ERPs.

- Teachers need to continue to scaffold, model and use mixed ability clinic groups to model ERP examples and practise specific skills related to ERP proposal forms and independent project research and work.

What do I do if I have a Grade 2/3 or Grade 2/3/4?

Any grade level has children with a diverse range of development, maturity, needs and strengths. It is true however, that these differences can seem especially disparate in a Grade 2/3 class, as the cohort will be straddling early childhood development and middle primary years. Many Grade 3 children, while technically of a particular chronological age and year level, may not yet be ready for an ERP, while some Grade 2 children (although probably not many) may be ready to take on a version of an ERP towards the end of the year.

We generally recommend that a Grade 2/3 combination uses a mix of investigations and ERPs (see *Play Matters 2nd Edition*). The investigation time would become the ERP time for those students working on an actual ERP. Tuning in would occur as for a P–2 class, and students working on a project would simply be a focus each fortnight like the other children. A Grade 2/3 classroom would be set up similarly to a P–2 classroom to ensure a rich range of experiences and resources which accommodate all aspects of students' learning, abilities and maturity.

The whole point of the WLA is that it draws on developmentally appropriate practices which aim to ensure that student learning is personalised and enhanced to accommodate and meet individual needs and abilities, regardless of chronological age or which grade students technically are in.

What about students who never choose to join an optional clinic group?

Once students have the modelling of other peers and see that some of the optional clinic groups are fun and interesting, they often do voluntarily sign up to attend a clinic group. The key here is that the compulsory clinic groups are the teacher's insurance clause to ensure that all students are attending specific learning opportunities in small and whole group instruction. Often the fact that they finally have a legitimate choice means they are more likely than in the past to join in. Sometimes inviting them to run an optional clinic group helps them to move away from their past resistance or hesitation.

Won't having the children check in at the communication board each day take too long?

It is amazing how quickly children adapt to new expectations, especially when they feel a little grown up and independent. In the early days of implementation, we recommend that teachers sit with the children at the communication board and work their way through the daily clinic groups, model filling in their diary, checking the timetable, inviting ideas for the ideas section and the classroom meeting agenda so that students are formally taught how to use, refer to and place in their diaries what is expected each day. Some days, very little will be needed to be placed in the diary.

Does the WLA work with just one teacher in a traditional classroom? How do we run clinic groups with just one teacher?

Yes, the WLA originally commenced with one-teacher classrooms in traditionally sized classrooms which are often quite small. Clinic groups are conducted just as small reading groups or teacher focus groups would be run in a classroom while other students are working independently. Teachers in one-teacher classrooms are encouraged to ask principals, parents and other community members to attend and conduct clinic groups at least once a week so that students are receiving modelling that not only teachers teach!

How does the WLA work in a team-teaching or open classroom situation?

Many schools now have open classrooms where a number of teachers and students share the space. The WLA is most effective in this situation.

Each home group of students still has their own communication board to check in with daily and each home group still meets for the morning tuning in, diary checks and setting the scene for the day.

During ERP time, it is often desirable to have all home groups working at ERPs at the same time. This makes it easier during the immersion phase where the cohort may all visit on an excursion or be shown a video or have a guest speaker attend. It also means that one teacher may run a clinic group for any students across the cohort during ERP time. Clinic groups in any subject areas can also be shared by a number of teachers including literacy and numeracy if that suits the teachers.

The key is that each group has and retains their own home group teacher and tuning in and reflection time and that each home group has their own individual classroom meeting.

Can we just combine what we already do in terms of class meetings and discussions?

You might be able to if you can accommodate the agenda being contributed to by the students and if you ensure that it is not a meeting about behaviours or attitudes, but rather a general meeting about life events, global issues and general discussion which from time to time may include (but not be dominated by) in-house issues.

The students are finding the ERP proposals difficult. Can we simplify or modify the proposal form for the ERPs?

No. The proposal form has been specially trialled and tested with a large range of students. As described in Chapter 4, the completion of the proposal form is an integral part of the teaching and learning process. It requires teacher input, modelling and support with students. It is *not* intended that the proposal form is a quick one-hour, fill-in-the-box type of tool where students complete it on their own. Modifying or simplifying the ERP proposal will compromise a core element of the approach.

Do we have focus students, tuning in and reflection each day even when we have ERP time?

Yes. The idea is that the class tunes in and reflects on learning each day regardless of whether or not there is ERP time scheduled. This also ensures that links to learning across subject areas are modelled each day.

Appendices

Term Subject Focus and Key Learning Intentions

Term: **Subject focus:**

Subject description or focus areas (taken from framework):
-

Key learning intentions identified:
For the students to:
-

the Walker Learning Approach
DEVELOPMENTALLY APPROPRIATE PRACTICE

Statement of Intent
Grades 3–6

		Term:	Subject focus:		
		Key learning intentions identified: For the students to: •			
		Commencing date:		**Weeks:**	
Developmental domain focus	**Learning outcomes (state/national framework)**	**Immersion or other exposure, concepts, excursions, school events**	**Assessment/ reflection experiences**	**Learning experiences**	**Modifications**
Emotional For the students to: •	*Numeracy* For the students to: •	•	•	•	•
Social For the students to: •	*Literacy* For the students to: •	*Students' interests* •			
Language For the students to: •	*Other subjects* For the students to: •				
Cognitive/Thinking For the students to: •					
Physical/Health For the students to: •					

Engagement Matters © Kathy Walker and Shona Bass 2011

Appendices | **91**

Focus Student Roster		
Day	**Date**	**Name**
Monday		• • •
Tuesday		• • •
Wednesday		• • •
Thursday		• • •
Friday		• • •
Monday		• • •
Tuesday		• • •
Wednesday		• • •
Thursday		• • •
Friday		• • •

Engagement Matters © Kathy Walker and Shona Bass 2011

Clinic Group Timetable

Day	Session	Type of Clinic
Monday	•	•
Tuesday	•	•
Wednesday	•	•
Thursday	•	•
Friday	•	•

Engagement Matters © Kathy Walker and Shona Bass 2011

Compulsory Clinic Group

Title:
Date:
Time:
Conducted by:
Description:
Maximum participants:
Student's name:
Student's name:
Student's name:
Student's name:
Student's name:
Student's name:

Compulsory Clinic Group

Title:
Date:
Time:
Conducted by:
Description:
Maximum participants:
Student's name:
Student's name:
Student's name:
Student's name:
Student's name:
Student's name:

Engagement Matters © Kathy Walker and Shona Bass 2011

Optional Clinic Group

Title:	
Date: Time:	
Conducted by:	
Description:	
Maximum participants:	
Student's name:	
Student's name:	
Student's name:	
Student's name:	
Student's name:	
Student's name:	

Optional Clinic Group

Title:	
Date: Time:	
Conducted by:	
Description:	
Maximum participants:	
Student's name:	
Student's name:	
Student's name:	
Student's name:	
Student's name:	
Student's name:	

Engagement Matters © Kathy Walker and Shona Bass 2011

Individual Record
Teacher's Notes

Student name: **Grade:**

Development/Behaviour

Observations:
-

Goals:
-

Key learning areas

Literacy observations/comments:
-

Literacy goals:
-

Numeracy observations/comments:
-

Numeracy goals:
-

Other learning observations/comments:
-

Goals:
-

Interests/ERP:
-

Other comments/observations:
-

Engagement Matters © Kathy Walker and Shona Bass 2011

Individual Record
Student/Parent Contributions

Student contributions

-

Parent contributions

-

Engagement Matters © Kathy Walker and Shona Bass 2011

Education Research Project (ERP) Student Proposal

Student name: Term: Date:

Project Scope

Major subject focus	
Key interest area	
Why are you interested?	
How does your interest link to the subject focus and learning intentions?	
What are you hoping to find out?	
Suggested timeline	
Will you be working in a team or on your own?	
What is your reason for choosing to work alone or in a team?	
In which ways will you present your project?	
Ways in which the project may be useful to others (will it have a link to the community?)	

Additional Learning

What aspects of literacy will be included in your project?	
What aspects of numeracy will be included in your project?	
Any other subject areas or skills that will be included in your project?	
List your personal goals for this project	
What skills do you already have that will help you with this project?	
Are there any challenges or difficulties you can think of that are related to this project?	

Engagement Matters © Kathy Walker and Shona Bass 2011

Education Research Project (ERP) Contract

Date:

I _____ agree to the terms and conditions of this contract as set out in my final proposal for the project titled '_____'.

Date when proposal was finalised	
Date of project completion	
Student's name	
Student's signature	
Teacher's name	
Teacher's signature	

Engagement Matters © Kathy Walker and Shona Bass 2011

Education Research Project (ERP) Assessment Guide

	Assessment	
Proposal preparation, consideration and completion		
Timeline		
Student-led conference		
Personal goals		
Project goals and intentions achieved		
Peer assessment		
ERP artefact artwork		

Engagement Matters © Kathy Walker and Shona Bass 2011

Learning Intentions
Student Version

Term:	
Subject focus	•
Learning intentions	•

Fortnight:	
For the students to...	
Literacy	•
Numeracy	•
Other subjects or programs	•

Engagement Matters © Kathy Walker and Shona Bass 2011

References

Alexander, R, Armstrong, M, Flutter, J, Hargreaves, L, Harrison, D, Harlen, W Hartley-Brewer, E, Kershner, R, Macbeath, J, Mayall, B, Northen, S, Pugh, G, Richards, C & Utting, D 2009, *Children, their world, their education: Final report and recommendations of the Cambridge Primary Review*, Routledge, London.

Bandura, A 1997, *Self efficacy: The exercise of control*, WH Freeman, New York.

Black, P & Wiliam, D 1998, 'Assessment and classroom learning', *Assessment in Education: Principles, policy and practice*, vol. 5, no. 1, pp. 7–74.

Bornholt, LJ 2005, *ASK-KIDS Inventory for children*, ACER Press, Camberwell, Victoria.

Copple, C & Bredekamp, S (eds) 2009, *Developmentally appropriate practice in early childhood programs: Serving children from birth through age 8*, National Association for the Education of Young Children, Washington DC.

Department of Education, Employment and Training 2002, *Middle Years Research and Development (MYRAD) Project: A report to the learning and teaching innovation division by the Centre for Applied Educational Research, Faculty of Education, The University of Melbourne*, State Government Victoria, Melbourne.

Edith Cowan University 2008, *Executive summary*, The Pipeline Project, Department of Education and Training, Perth, http://www.pipelineproject.org.au/

Edwards, C, Gandini, L & Forman, G (eds) 1998, *The hundred languages of children: The Reggio Emilia approach*, Ablex Publishing, Westport, Connecticut.

Fisher, JP & Glenister, JM 1992, *The Hundred Pictures Naming Test*, 2nd edn, ACER Press, Camberwell, Victoria.

Fisher, K 2006, *Proposed planning principles: Linking pedagogy and space*, Department of Education and Training, Victoria, http://www.eduweb.vic.gov.au/edulibrary/public/propman/facility/linking_pedagogy_and_space.pdf

Goeke, JL 2008, *Explicit instruction: Strategies for meaningful direct teaching*, Pearson Education, London.

Gresham, FM & Elliott, SN 2008, *Social skills improvement system*, PsychCorp, Circle Pines.

Jones, E & Reynolds, G 1992, *The play's the thing: Teachers' roles in children's play*, Teachers College Press, New York.

Livingston, MJ, McClain, BR & DeSpain, BC 1995, 'Assessing the consistency between teachers' philosophies and educational goals', *Education*, vol. 116, Fall, pp. 124–9.

Marion, R 2002, *Leadership in education: Organizational theory for the practitioner*, Waveland Press, Long Grove, Illinois.

Mazzuno, R 2001, *Leading to change: Teaching beyond subjects and standards*, John Wiley & Sons, Indianapolis, Indiana.

Miller, E & Almon, J 2009, *Crisis in the kindergarten: Why children need to play in school*, Alliance for Childhood, College Park, Maryland.

Naylor, S & Keogh, B 1999, 'Constructivism in the classroom: Theory into practice', *Journal of Science Teacher Education*, vol. 10, no. 2, pp. 93–106.

Pairman, A & Terreni, L 2001, *If the environment is the third teacher, what language does she speak?* Ministry of Education, New Zealand, http://www.educate.ece.govt.nz/learning/curriculumAndLearning/Learningenvironments/ThirdTeacher.aspx

Slavin, RE 1990, *Cooperative learning: Theory, research and practice*, Prentice Hall, Englewood Cliffs, New Jersey.

Strike, K & Posner, G 1985, 'A conceptual change view of learning and understanding', in L West & A Pines (eds), *Cognitive structure and conceptual change*, Academic Press, New York, pp. 211–31.

Summers, L (ed.) 1994, *Quality in teaching and learning: Making it happen*, Edith Cowan University, Perth.

Time, Learning and Afterschool Task Force 2007, *A new day for learning*, Charles Stewart Mott Foundation, Flint, Michigan, http://www.edutopia.org/pdfs/ANewDayforLearning.pdf

Walker, K 2009, *Executive summary: Research findings related to the implementation of the Australian developmental curriculum*, Early Life Foundations, Elwood, Victoria, http://walkerlearning.com.au/info/research-reports-the-australian-developmental-curriculum

Walker, K 2011, *Play matters*, 2nd edn, ACER Press, Camberwell, Victoria.

Weinstock, HR, Starr, RJ & Fazzaro, CJ, 1974, 'Comparing secondary teachers on logical consistency in educational philosophy and flexibility in teaching', *Instructional Science*, vol. 3, no. 2, pp. 115–26.

Wragg, EC 1997, *Assessment and learning in the primary school*, Routledge, New York.

Index

Entries in *italics* refer to figures or tables

assessment, 26, 59, 60, 66–73; traditional views of, 66; assessment rubric, *71*

boys, 4, 14

'checking in' (with communication board), 18–19, 27, 87
class meetings, 22, 24, *25*, 88
clinic groups, 19–22, *23*, 87; during ERP time, 49; pro forma, 59–60; timetable, *60*
communication board, 17–19, 27, 84, 87
contracts (for ERPs), 48, 61
cost of implementation, 86

definition of terms, 9
development of children, 2, 5–7
developmentally appropriate practice, *7*, 7–8, 14, 15; and mixed grades, 87
documentation *see* planning, documentation and reporting

educational research projects *see* ERPs
electronic media, 19
ERPs (educational research projects), 25, 42–52, 61, 88; benefits, 42; key points, 45; assessment rubric, *71*
expo, 25, 51–2, 72

focus student roster, 50, 59
focus students, 19, 27–8, 42, 49, 50, 86, 88

immersion (phase of ERP), 46–7, 49, 50–1

implementation of WLA, 32–8, 84, 85, 86, 87
individual records, 60, 72, 84
integrated studies topic *see* topics
issues for educators, 5

leadership, role of, 10, 32–4, *33*, 84, 86
learning environment, 16–17
learning intentions, 44, 45–6, 48, 50, 56, 57, *57*, 59, *59*, 85; student version, 61
literacy and numeracy: in WLA, 4, 14, 15, 16, 84–5; in clinic groups, 20, 21; in ERPs, 25, 42, *47*, 78, 79, 80; learning intentions, 56, 57, *59*

mentoring, during implementation of WLA, 34–5, *35*, 36, 84, 85, 86

national tests *see* standardised testing
numeracy *see* literacy and numeracy

observation, 70

parent information, 34, *35*, 36–7, 84
parent interviews *see* student–teacher–parent interviews
pedagogy, defined, *9*
peer assessment, 69–70
philosophy, educational, 8–10
planning, documentation and reporting, 22, 25–6, 56–62; during implementation, 37–8
portfolio, student's, 61, 68–9, 72
professional development, 33, 34, *35*, 36, 38, 85, 86
proposal (for ERP), 42, *46*, 47, 51, 61, 88; developing, 76–80
proposal form, *46–7*, 47–8, 50, 51, 61, 76, 77–8, 88

record sheets, 61–2

reflection by students, 28, 49–50, 69, 88
reporting, 25–6, 60, 66–8, 70–3 *see also* planning, documentation and reporting
role of teacher in ERP process, 43, 50

school reports, 60, 72
self assessment, 26, 69
self reflection *see* reflection by students
SOI *see* statement of intent
standardised testing, 26, 67, 73
statement of intent (SOI), 57–9, *58*, *59*
student interests, links to subject focus and learning intentions, 45–6, 48, 76–80
student journal, 51
student-led conferencing, 19, 49, 50, 70, 72
student–teacher–parent interviews, 72, 84
subject focus, 44, 45–6, *46*, 48, 50, 56, *57*, 85

teacher's assistant, 19, 27
testing, limitations of, 66, 67, 69, 70
timeline, for ERPs, *46*, 50; for implementation of WLA, 36; for student portfolios, 69
timetable, 26–7, *26*, 61; for clinic groups, *60*
topics (of inquiry), distinguished from ERPs, 25, 42, 44, 85
'tuning in', 27, *27*, 43, 49, 88
typical day, 27–8
typical week, 16, 26, 28

weekly timetable *see* timetable
WLA (Walker Learning Approach); basis of, 2, 3, 4–5, 14; principles of, 14–15, 28; components of, 15–26; implementation of, 32–8

Play Matters
2nd Edition

Investigative learning for preschool to Grade 2

Kathy Walker

In the second edition of the highly successful resource, **Play Matters**, Kathy Walker demonstrates the key principles of the Walker Learning Approach that she has developed over 15 years of observation, participation and presentation in schools and child care centres across Australia.

Play Matters 2nd Edition continues to provide practical guidance and innovative strategies for teachers working with young children from preschool to Grade 2, through a unique balance of explicit instruction in literacy and numeracy skills and personalised, explorative learning. The book promotes the active engagement of all young children, with an enhanced focus on children from diverse backgrounds as well as children with specific needs.

Play Matters 2nd Edition is replete with pedagogical features to support implementation in any educational setting. It contains a full-colour section of photographs to highlight key themes, and downloadable template documents for planning, assessment and reporting activities. Organisational ideas and resources are provided, along with a bibliography for further reference and advice.